I0056788

OPTIMAL LEADERSHIP

REFLECTIONS OF A SERIAL CEO

WILF BLACKBURN

WITH

PHILIP WHITELEY

BREAKTHROUGH BOOKS

First published in Great Britain in 2025 by Breakthrough Books.

Print ISBN: 978-1-0687185-3-3

The rights of Wilf Blackburn and Philip Whiteley to be identified as the authors of this Work have been asserted by them in accordance with the Copyright, Designs and Patents Act 1988.

Copyright © 2025 by Wilf Blackburn and Philip Whiteley

All rights reserved.

No part of this book may be reproduced in any form or by any electronic or mechanical means, including information storage and retrieval systems, without written permission from the author, except for the use of brief quotations in a book review.

No part of this book has been written with the use or help of artificial intelligence. No part of this book may be used or reproduced to train artificial intelligence technologies or systems.

Cover design by Emma Allison. Book formatting by Ivy Ngeow. Illustrations by Judith Blackburn.

CONTENTS

FOREWORD

BY PROFESSOR ANDREW SCOTT

There must be far more books about leadership than there are leadership styles. Among the many insights of this excellent short volume, Wilf Blackburn provides a reason for that imbalance. Even though becoming CEO is seen as the pinnacle of a career, it isn't a position that has a clearly defined career path. The result is a need to think, learn, and adapt for the demands of this important role. To help you do so is Wilf's admirable aim. Backed up by his own experience across a range of countries and cultures, and supported by theory and evidence, this is what *Optimal Leadership* delivers.

There is much to like about the content of these pages. Form and content align splendidly. For a CEO, one of the constant tensions is to take a huge agenda with many moving parts and then focus on what really matters. The challenge is to not exclude important issues but also not to get bogged down in unnecessary detail. Wilf shows in each chapter what an excellent CEO he must have been, quickly getting to the heart of the matter, reviewing all sides and then reaching a conclusion with succinct and practical action points.

In doing so, Wilf's analysis reveals an obvious point about what you want in a book about leadership. Given the breadth of the challenge, you don't want a book that focuses on just one dimension and makes leadership sound easy. That will leave you ill-equipped for the challenge. But neither do you want a book that covers everything in such detail that it becomes an impractical guide. The book stresses the need for a leader to show 'intellectual nimbleness' and that attribute is admirably displayed throughout these pages. This is a book that covers all major issues that leaders face. It does so with clarity and focus, but all the time with an emphasis on clear, practical and actionable advice.

A striking feature of the book is how it brings clarity out of chaos, surely the hallmark of good leadership. It doesn't do so with a simple theoretical framework. Based, I suspect, on his experience, the author is too smart to believe in simple dogma. As the former heavyweight boxing champion Mike Tyson once remarked, 'Everyone has a plan until they get punched in the mouth.' Instead, it is through accepting ambiguity, and limits to what you can control, that effective leadership is to be found. Leadership isn't about an exclusive focus on business as usual or chasing radical change. Being a CEO is accepting that you are at the head of a hierarchy but also realising you are enmeshed in the heart of a web of complex relationships. It is about acting confidently but embracing humility. It is about directing people and resources but also stepping back and empowering people. It is about being ambitious but also knowing your limits. My own favourite is the advice to 'move slowly to become quicker'.

As Wilf shows, this isn't about contradictory calls to action or ducking decisions. Instead, it is through accepting and embracing these ambiguities that true leadership emerges. Being a leader requires accepting the tumult that occurs all around you and in its midst helping your organisation to succeed through high engagement and high performance. As the ancient Greek philosopher Heraclitus said, 'Nothing endures but change itself.' But accepting this doesn't mean that as a leader you are at the mercy of events or have to flip flop strategically from one issue to another, without taking a position. As this book stresses, there is one thing that is needed for a firm to succeed and which leadership has to bring about if it is to navigate forward – encouraging a culture that is collaborative and curious under wise leadership. How to do so, based on experience and principle, is what is distilled into these pages.

Wilf stresses the value in *Optimal Leadership* of 'responsible authority', of leadership that points in the right direction but does so in an empowering way. That is ultimately what this book does. Leadership isn't easy – organisations and the world are too complex for that to be the case. But, in embracing complexity and ambiguity, this book shows how you can achieve clarity and develop your own leadership style in an actionable way.

Leadership is hard and achieving success is even harder, but focusing on what you can do and how to get others to succeed with you is the hallmark of good leadership. After reading this book, you will be armed with the tools and questions to succeed but, above all, the confidence and clear-mindedness to tackle the task.

Andrew Scott
Professor of Economics
London Business School

PREFACE

Given the increasing pace of change in the economic world of the 21st Century, with characteristics commonly described by the acronym VUCA (volatile, uncertain, complex, ambiguous), senior executives and their organisations need to become increasingly nimble and adaptive. This involves a readiness to innovate and move quickly, often with a more team-based, less hierarchical form of organisation than those characterised by the traditional corporation.

Prioritising such strengths, however, can involve the risk of neglecting essential business disciplines: technical expertise; clear accountability; unambiguous decision-making; quality of service delivery; and regulatory compliance.

This book argues that a common framing of the challenge of organisational leadership as being either 'steady state' or 'radical disruption' is unhelpful, as it simplifies the issue into an unrealistic binary choice. In practice, an innovative agenda is often unpalatable to both the board and their newly appointed CEO, who is perhaps someone promoted to the role well into their career. For such an individual, an overly enthusiastic agenda of disruption, to 'move fast, shake the box and break things', can risk backfiring. Instead, the CEO errs on the side of caution – sometimes fatally so.

An alternative to these binary extremes is the 'optimal' leader, one who can combine strengths in strategy and operations with the ability to lead change programs. A CEO can and should apply elements of both continuity and change.

This book encourages CEOs to be courageous: to be bold and innovative where this is needed, and to do so in a smart way based on approaches that have proven to be effective. It offers a guide to optimising reliability and innovation. This approach does not necessarily mean compromise; it does mean capturing the best features of both. To do this, rather than calibrating the organisation by the pace with which it can change, it helps to nurture timeless qualitative features, such as the strength of collaboration, intellectual curiosity, practical wisdom, and the ability to acknowledge and correct mistakes. Strength in all these areas makes it more likely that the organisation will be intelligently nimble, adapting to technological, market and other changes, and testing and refining innovations while staying close to customers and their desires. A related key strength of CEOs is their ability to select and put together great leadership teams capable of accomplishing this.

Research evidence on organisational development by thinkers such as Peter Drucker and Jeffrey Pfeffer supports the conclusion that ultimately you achieve the most sustainable success by empowering and not exploiting the workforce – that you can do well by doing good. I was fortunate to learn the lessons of 'thought leaders' such as these early in my executive career and had the opportunity to apply them during two decades as a CEO. I discovered that their recommended approaches are highly effective – if anything, to a more significant degree than I had anticipated. Moreover, they are effective through all phases of a business's development and will build the organisational resilience required to deal with major shocks.

This leads to a puzzle, one that this book seeks to address.

Given the long-established evidence base linking a healthy employment culture with high performance, why are such practices still far from universal? It is a common experience to encounter highly intelligent senior managers, successful in many aspects of commercial management, who neglect crucial aspects of leading people, such as developing teams and attending to communication. These are vitally important for there to be sustained effectiveness. In some cases, these matters are pejoratively – and inaccurately – referred to as the 'soft stuff'. The concept of the optimal leader applies to an equal balance of commercial and people-related intelligence, neither of which is 'soft'.

So, I make no apology for adding to the considerable literature on the empowered workplace. Yes, there are thousands of books making similar points, yet there is a collective failure of global business leadership teams to adopt the evidence base as comprehensively as, say, the medical profession upholds the evidence base in epidemiology. Chapters 8 and 9 discuss some of the reasons for this and make some proposals that are hopefully constructive.

This book is supported by evidence but is practical in its content. It contains advice for the individual CEO, such as how to go about your first 100 days and how to structure senior leadership team meetings to get the best out of them. It aims to offer an experience-based masterclass on how to meet the needs of customers, employees, board members, media, shareholders and, where necessary, regulators.

Optimal Leadership arose from an endeavour to critically reflect on my CEO-ship. The book distils reflections from my experiences in many roles across several geographies for more than three decades into my 'manifesto' of CEO practices.

Whilst not a memoir, the suggested leadership practices included are based solely on 'recipes I've cooked' and modified multiple times, and which I believe are worthwhile retaining. I suspect that many of the practices included are sufficiently generic to be effective in multiple geographies, business sectors, organisational types and periods in time.

I hope that these 'recipes' will be useful to others, particularly those who either aspire to assume a CEO (or other organisational leadership) role or who have already done so, whilst encouraging debate about the practice of being a CEO.

Wilf Blackburn

PART ONE

CHAPTER 1
THE FIRST 100 DAYS

A company is neither a structure nor a hierarchy. It is a network of relationships, held together by trust and reciprocal economic dependencies and incentives. If you are appointed CEO, it helps to understand this. You do not sit at the apex of a pyramid, but rather at the centre of a set of interconnected webs of relationships and influences. Moreover, this complex set of networks is continually changing, from one day to the next. It is too complex, multi-dimensional and fluid to be described accurately by an organisational chart, although such visual aids can help clarify lines of accountability.

An essential first discipline for the incoming CEO, therefore, is to understand what the organisation is before putting in place measures to improve it. This book is aimed at showing how a CEO can create an innovative, adaptive organisation that is also one that delivers consistently in line with the company's promises to the customer. It is pragmatic, primarily describing the practices that have been found to be effective, rather than the features of an idealised nimble and innovative business.

This book takes creativity and innovation as a given: they are a must, especially as markets and technologies change so rapidly. Too often in business literature, these features are described as inputs, yet in my experience they are better understood as outcomes. It doesn't work just to ask people to be creative and innovative. What's most effective in practice is to have the right conversations, meeting styles and arrangements that permit people – most of whom are by nature curious and innovative and want to help the business succeed – to bring their creativity to the workplace.

Conditions for permitting and encouraging innovation and creativity include the following: tolerating mistakes; encouraging experimentation; bringing in people with different approaches; and allowing people to begin a project without having the full answer before they commence. Techniques to encourage these healthy disciplines will feature in later chapters, especially in Part 2, which covers organisational culture. It is helpful to keep them in mind when planning steps for the first weeks in a post. It is the culture of the organisation that delivers – or fails to deliver. The rest of this chapter describes proven steps that help the incoming CEO establish a healthy, innovative culture.

Two paradoxical concepts that inform such preparations are *functional humility* and *moving slow to become quick*.

Functional humility – to enhance your influence it helps to understand its limitations. As CEO, you can actually achieve very little on your own; by harnessing the skills, experience and capabilities of everyone in the enterprise, you can become highly successful.

Move slow to become fast – take your time to understand and develop trusting and engaging relationships. This will enable you to build teams that can respond quickly and decisively, with the autonomy and capability to respond to emerging needs and changing context, guided by an overall strategy and sense of purpose.

First meetings: functional heads

The first meetings to call are one-to-one briefings with the organisation's senior leaders, to understand their issues and strengths and gauge their readiness for new strategies. It helps if those responsible for a certain area acknowledge the issues that need addressing in their function or specialism, and volunteer to help lead improvements. If the CEO simply instructs the change in their area before gathering in-depth intelligence or seeking the engagement of the executive, the psychological dynamic becomes one of punishment or reward, and progress is hampered. This may be necessary in the case of significant under-performance, but it is a last resort; better to engage in discussions based on open questions to discern the pressing issues and priorities (see **Key Themes and Questions**).

These one-to-one meetings also serve as an opportunity to get to know the individual, what is important to them, and what are their immediate objectives and longer-term ambitions. Assuming that they are a good fit and well-motivated, this process enables the incoming CEO to engage with the individual to ensure that they have sufficient resources to meet their objectives, and in turn that these objectives help the enterprise to deliver.

So, the first priority for an incoming CEO is setting up these individual meetings, one-to-ones, with the leaders who comprise your team. They are typically fearful, uncertain as to whether they will remain part of the team with a change of leader. Usually, the team will be around seven or eight people at that level. First and foremost, learning about what's important to them both in business and as people is effective.

There is a great line by Maya Angelou: "People don't care how much you know until they know how much you care." Your new team might not have researched you in advance, even when you have moved in from another country within the organisation. They are in their own world so they don't really think that much about you and what you might bring. Even inside an organisation, you have to start all over again, every time – just finding out what's important to people, what they are working on, what their objectives are.

This initial round of one-to-one meetings is also used to gauge the strength of teamwork and collaboration among the senior executives; whether there have been major disagreements, either due to inter-personal conflict or genuine disagreement over business issues. An incoming leader needs to have a grasp of the emotional and political territory, and how to wield influence responsibly to resolve disputes, facilitate conversations and achieve compromises. The ultimate aim is to ensure that the whole enterprise is focused productively on the operational and strategic priorities.

Key themes and questions for initial one-to-one meetings

- Let's talk about you – who you are, not what you do.
- Tell me about your family.
- What are the most important areas of interest to you outside work?

Regarding work:

- What are your objectives this year and what are you aiming to accomplish?
- If you weren't constrained, for example by resources, what else would you wish to build?
- What are the constraints that you are faced with and how might we overcome them?
- What would be the benefits of building our capabilities at a faster pace?
- Tell me about your team.

Next round of meetings: operational and strategic discussions

The next step is to hold an operational and strategic meeting to identify emerging issues. This will enable you to decide which of the internal leaders will be willing and able to lead any changes required, and who might be holding the organisation back. Accelerating the pace of change without these preliminary steps to secure engagement from the managerial team risks loss of momentum, or even sabotage.

The intelligence gathered at the initial round of one-to-one meetings will inform you on how to deal with individuals: whether to nurture or challenge; when to listen and when to volunteer an opinion or suggest a course of action; and when to ask for more data or other information. There are often dominant issues, or a significant matter such as a local crisis, that need to be urgently addressed.

Key themes and questions for initial operational and strategic meetings

- How are we performing against our objectives for this year and how will we finish the year?
- How does this align with the expectations of our stakeholders, including our employees?
- How shall we prioritise our efforts to obtain the best overall result this year?
- Is there anything about the way we work that is either contributing to or hindering our performance, and how can we address this?
- Longer term, where do we wish the company to be?
- Who will be our target customers and what will be our proposition to them?
- What is holding us back from executing this vision faster?
- Why is the ambition so small?
- Let's look at ourselves against our competitors through the lens of the Customer Value Curve approach in *Blue Ocean Strategy*[i]. What are the gaps between where we are and our aspiration?
- What shall we stop doing?
- Who are the star performers in the next levels of leadership? Are they in roles that are business critical in relation to our priorities? How are we developing them?

Immediate priorities

For many incoming CEOs there is a key priority, in some cases a 'burning platform'. This is especially the case in a forced succession, where the appointment of the new CEO may have been prompted by a sudden departure, perhaps due to under-performance in a part or parts of the enterprise. While the previous incumbent may have lost their position as a result of a crisis, even in a carefully planned succession there will often be a dominant issue to be addressed.

The 'burning platform' may be initially somewhat hidden – for example, an emerging issue to do with an under-performing product line within an otherwise profitable company. In this context, the CEO may have to confront complacency, or lack of clarity on financial information, and insist that the organisation confronts the issue to head off a potential crisis. Rigour and strength of analysis are essential to identify such an issue correctly and prioritise it.

With a specific crisis to attend to, especially one that is high-profile, there is a danger that the incoming CEO will devote almost all his or her time to this single issue. While it is important to both recognise and address the problem, it is rarely the case that everyone in the organisation is being impacted – it may just be a technology issue, or a problem with manufacturing. Therefore, be mindful at all times of the needs of the organisation as a whole. Accordingly, you should pay sufficient immediate attention to the crisis then broaden your attention as quickly as possible. Ultimately, it is important that the organisation appreciates that the new CEO isn't simply a trouble-shooter in a specific area, but rather someone with a genuine appreciation of the entire business.

Strength of the managerial team

The exploratory discussions of the first weeks in post may yield uncomfortable information: some senior individuals may be under-performing; some may be hiding information for reasons that are to do with internal politics. A later chapter will focus on the central importance of hiring the right people and managing the wrong individuals out of the organisation, including advice on how to do so whilst minimising disruption or harm to the individual and hopefully guiding them towards a more suitable role.

Smart hiring and firing policies should be based on a foundation of strong and accurate intelligence on the existing organisation.

An obvious challenge for an incoming CEO who is new to the organisation is rapidly learning about its culture, key personnel, strengths, and weaknesses. The round of interviews and other meetings become an important process of intelligence-gathering. For an internally promoted individual, the challenges are more subtle: they will already have a good knowledge of the culture and key features of the organisation, but they may find that the information is less complete than they supposed. Also, if the new CEO previously headed a function – such as finance, or marketing – they will be subliminally associated with that department for some time after appointment as CEO. This presents two challenges – firstly, the CEO will have to successfully perform a major reorientation towards leading the enterprise as a whole. Secondly, they will need to be seen by the wider employee population to have made this reorientation to leading the whole organisation.

Summary

It may be an exaggeration to say that a CEO's first 100 days determine whether the tenure will be a success. Individuals can recover from an unfortunate start or build influence effectively over a longer duration. However, experience shows that a strong start helps build a foundation for effective leadership. A common metaphorical exhortation for this period is that the new leader should 'hit the ground running'. It is perhaps not the best metaphor, as it is not appropriate to hit anything; nor is it to run, at least not immediately. Whilst counter-intuitive, this advice is especially relevant if you are planning significant radical changes. For this, you will need the support and engagement of key players throughout the enterprise, and this requires some patience and care in the early weeks, without being too deliberate or slow.

CHAPTER 2
THE CEO AS A PROFESSION

C uriously, for the most senior executive role within an organisation, there isn't a standard, universal career path that prepares an individual to become the Chief Executive Officer. Combining the optimal blend of behaviours, attributes and knowledge base required for the role is difficult because they must be assembled from a variety of sources in different ways over an extended period of time. This development is necessarily eclectic and can be challenging to maintain while heading a specialist function, which is often the role one occupies for some years before becoming a CEO. There is a need for multiple learning experiences and the chance to build personal resources.

This lack of a career path appears to be a structural weakness in business management, one that probably hampers implementation of the evidence base on the importance of an empowered workforce, featuring an optimal balance in executives between commercial capability and the ability to manage people.

The CEO role isn't a 'CXO-plus' role – it is significantly and qualitatively different from heading a specialist function, even a large department in a major corporation. The development required for a CEO is an equal blend of knowledge (on business, markets, technology and so on); and personal leadership qualities (the ability to build effective teams and harness the ability of each team member), and the ability to ensure that the enterprise as a whole collaborates effectively.

The MBA is perhaps the closest to being a qualification for the CEO. It covers essential disciplines, combining strategic awareness, market analysis, financial analysis and operational ability. Ideally, to ensure relevance to current technology and market conditions, an MBA would be undertaken by individuals when they have gained more experience, rather than happening several years or even decades before they are likely to become CEOs. In an interim period between qualification and appointment to a CEO role, they are typically rising within the ranks of a certain functional discipline. This experience equips them more directly for the role of heading these functions, rather than being the senior executive of all of them.

Business schools and many employers have faced criticism for over-emphasising the knowledge base and neglecting the ability to coach and handle people. Changes in curricula and the growth of the coaching industry have balanced this to some degree, although there is still an observable imbalance in many businesses, with a focus on short-term results and commercial targets over empowerment and teams. The development required for an effective CEO is eclectic, but the business school curricula and typical career experience can be quite narrow, with the consequence that a CEO needs to be self-taught to a significant degree. Chapter 5 discusses the discipline of continual learning in more depth, while Chapters 8 and 9 discuss the importance of the highly engaged workforce.

It's not about being the best

A CEO must understand how the whole enterprise functions. They must know how the various specialisms need to be skilfully choreographed, or how the CEO is like a conductor of an orchestra. Whilst these metaphors lack precision, they are closer to the reality than a linear model of strategy-execution-processes-targets. A business is much more than just a list of objectives and tasks. The need to be more of a coordinator than a dictator is only made more important by the volatility in markets and by rapid technological changes that require continual innovation and adaptability. This is not a newly discovered requirement: most successful long-lasting businesses have had to adapt, sometimes rapidly. The effective CEO seeks to establish a nimble, innovative business through nurturing a healthy culture of learning, inquiry, experimentation and iteration.

The concept of the CEO as akin to a choreographer or conductor is significant. The most effective senior executives are not autocrats; they do, however, wield considerable decision-making responsibility and are accountable directly to the board. The central insight of the effective CEO is this: *You need to nurture the best, not be the best.*

To take an analogy from sports, the most brilliantly talented individuals on the field are not always the most effective team coaches. These are different, complementary abilities. In business, if there are colleagues more brilliant than the CEO at understanding new markets, developing software, devising sales strategies, or using AI to improve marketing, then you have the makings of a world-class team.

An ambitious CEO, or an aspiring CEO, may instinctively feel a need to demonstrate their intellectual superiority; and, indeed, they do in many ways require a high level of cognitive ability. However, the *types* of intelligence required are more nuanced and subtle than may be immediately apparent. It is not about simply having advanced analytical skills, but rather the capability to put a team together, understand how the whole enterprise collaborates, and manage the dynamics involved. Otherwise, there's a risk that a team of many talented individuals will become less than the sum of its parts, or – in the worst cases – become divided and conflicted with each other. The issue of delegating and leading through the team is discussed further in Chapter 3.

Insights for aspiring executives: Spiral upwards

As discussed in Chapter 1, the first weeks in post as CEO can be daunting. It is not ideal if this is the first time that you are grappling with the complexity of how different specialist functions need to be coordinated. A strong recommendation is that an aspiring executive gains experience in more than one discipline; also, ideally, in more than one sector, geographical region and size of enterprise. The CEO should 'spiral upwards', rather than aim for vertical ascent.

For example, the mindset and priorities of a head of supply chain will be different from those of a head of marketing. It helps enormously to have more than superficial knowledge of the different approaches required for different parts of a business. One of the least obvious but necessary attributes of a skilful executive is empathy. This is a quality more often associated with a therapist or a coach, and we might think that decisiveness is more appropriate for the executive leader. However, the ability to understand how the impacts of a decision on one part of the enterprise might be sensitively adapted to suit a new strategy or way of working can be of great value. Empathy supplies you with a form of organisational intelligence.

If there are limited opportunities to gain full-time managerial experiences in different sectors, functions or regions, there are still ways to 'spiral upwards' to gain different experiences. Examples include volunteering for leading cross-functional initiatives, or being a representative on a board of a non-profit entity. Within an organisation, there may be an opportunity to lead an internal project team. For example, the project manager for software development may be someone from outside IT, representing either the external or internal customer. Putting oneself forward for such opportunities is an excellent way of building leadership muscle.

There may, however, be an advantage in becoming a CEO at a relatively early career stage, rather than towards the end of your career. For example, if after 15 years or so heading marketing or finance you have been able to gain diverse experiences, learning how the different disciplines work effectively together – and how to facilitate the necessary conversations that lead to the best solutions or compromises – you will have an effective grounding and may arrive early to senior leadership. Those with the aptitude to become CEOs are often those who are curious about specialisms other than their own, who are keen to seek diverse experiences, and who are interested in learning how the whole entity cooperates, as well as how the specialist function excels.

Insights for organisations: Rotation, rotation, rotation
Some corporations have sought to develop rounded leaders by adopting an approach of rotation, so that individuals being prepared for the CEO role have direct experience of more than one function. For the CEO seeking to encourage such rotation, one effective tactic is to reward those managers who are prepared to try new roles within the organisation after three or four years. Individuals tend to maximise their learning and achievements within five years of taking on a managerial role. The employer brand is better sold as an offer of a great learning environment, rather than the source of a job for life.

Are there risks with rotation? May it potentially deplete essential specialist functions of adequate specialist knowledge and experience? Clearly, there is a balance to be struck between developing future leaders and maintaining operations. The head of risk doesn't want anything blowing up, and that's the number one priority. However, if there's enough strength in depth in the functions, then you can move out a leader, creating space to bring in a different leader from elsewhere or to let somebody move up and assume more responsibility. You can't usually do this with start-ups, but generally the benefits of rotation – of bringing in new people – with the refresh that this encourages, outweigh the risks.

A responsible enterprise must have sound financial controls, risk management and other checks and balances, all of which constrain the potential for experimentation and for giving executive experience to aspiring managers. However, a policy of neglecting long-term leadership development also comes with risk. The role is all about building a sustainable business and it is costly to hire external CEOs.

In one role as regional CEO with an international firm, I was overseeing 16 business units, each of which had a local CEO role. This afforded the opportunity to allow relatively inexperienced but very capable executives to step up. Given the controls and level of overview in place, this was a low-risk way of giving promising managers real CEO responsibility relatively early in their executive careers.

Rotation and early promotion can be highly rewarding policies, but they should be sensitively managed. Too much churn can cause operational problems; a manager who leaves may take their whole team with them. An enterprise does require a long organisational memory – but this does not have to reside within an individual, provided there are ways of sharing and saving important narratives and lessons. Overall, if implemented with sensitivity and the benefit of experience, the risks of rotation are low while the rewards can be considerable.

Profile of an effective CEO

There isn't a short-cut to becoming a CEO, and there isn't a diploma that qualifies you. That said, the role shouldn't be reserved only for those near the end of their executive career; the optimal blend of experience and intellectual development can be acquired at a relatively early stage. Personal attributes are important; in particular, there is an optimal blend of decisiveness combined with a capacity for empathy, which may be relatively rare or prove difficult to achieve.

Key Attributes

- Curiosity and continual learning
- Judgement
- Balancing consensus and decisiveness
- Managing relationships, including the ability to build teams
- Gauging the internal dynamics
- Rigour and subjecting ideas to a pragmatic test: does it add value?
- Distinguishing between a promising idea and a fad
- The ability to both learn and recover from mistakes

CHAPTER 3
LEADERSHIP THROUGH THE TEAM

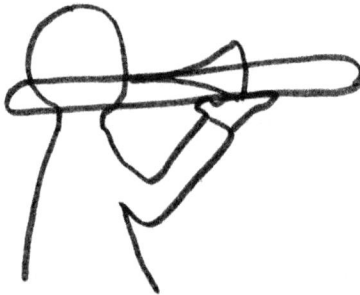

M any high-flying young managers who begin learning the art of executive management have landed a promising post at a major corporation and secured a place on an MBA program at a prestigious international business school. It is a logical conclusion to assume that, in order to progress to CEO, they will have to demonstrate that their intellectual accomplishments and understanding of business and markets are superior to those of others on the course, or of their fellow managers in the workplace.

Once at the apex of an organisation, their high level of analytical and strategic ability will enable them to guide the enterprise in the most profitable direction.

However, this is not how the most effective CEOs work in practice. They undergo a sobering, but ultimately empowering, discovery that executive management is a highly collaborative process. It involves the effective coordination of talent, not the imperious direction of will; of being the orchestral conductor who must coax high performance rather than simply demand that it happens. Not being the best may even be an advantage. Rather, you learn that ultimately your most important role is to be the best at getting the best out of others. Ambitious, highly intelligent executives could believe, if perhaps tacitly, that their objective is to become omniscient – that they ought to possess the answers to any commercial problem they may face. In practice, this is neither possible nor desirable.

You learn that everything in business is done by teams, even in the smallest start-ups, and certainly at major corporations. The role of the CEO involves understanding the strengths of the team members, ensuring they are allocated the most suitable roles, and working hard to ensure that the communication and sense of common purpose are strong. Some of the most effective executives are perfectly relaxed about not being 'the best', as defined by certain indicators such as top of the MBA class or having the highest IQ. Above all, they don't give up because they cannot be the best. Some people drop out because they can't be number one; they'll stop playing a musical instrument, for example, because they know they will never get to play at the highest level. Highly effective CEOs see themselves as being committed to continual improvement, and to getting the best out of others. They can facilitate and coach individuals and teams, as well as taking the lead and making tough decisions. They learn that others' ways of thinking, and the knowledge and intelligence of other managers, represent valuable resources, so they appoint brilliant people to the right roles and motivate them to perform. The focus becomes the intended outcome – for customers and for the business – rather than individuals gaining the credit. This shared sense of commitment and achievement becomes the ethic in a business with high-performing teams. In turn, organisations work most effectively if the heads of functions also delegate, debate, share knowledge, and focus on desired outcomes, rather than guarding their area of expertise as something on which only they are qualified to speak.

Paul Simons, a former colleague and HR leader, describes how the team ethic works in practice:

"For me, [the role] is about partnering with the business and getting business outcomes. It's never really been my goal to be recognised as the best HR person but to be recognised by my colleagues from other functions as being able to contribute towards delivering a common goal."

Such an approach does involve a personal challenge, because in this democratic spirit where other members of the team feel permitted to have a strong view on your area of expertise, sometimes they may make a valid point and at other times they may not. Paul adds:

"I'm a human being – I have some ego. And so there are times when I'm thinking, well, I know this – I'm the expert. Or even worse, oh my goodness, I'm going to be judged because I should be the expert, and the company is paying me … [But] what I learned, [was that] no one cared about who had the knowledge. We cared about the outcome."

A 'servant leader' must still be a leader

This emphasis on facilitating and coaching as a leader, rather than being an autocrat, has at times been described by the catchy, counter-intuitive title of 'servant leadership', which is similar to the concept of functional humility mentioned in Chapter 1. Terms such as *servant* and *humility* need to be qualified and used with care, as they imply deference and could be associated with a lack of decisiveness. While learning to display some humility is a helpful corrective for those accustomed to making executive decisions, there are others who need to become more assertive when they are sure of their ground, or when a decision needs to be made to avoid letting an important issue drift.

Much depends on the starting point, hence the emphasis in this book on being optimal. There is an element of deference involved in leadership, which can involve deferring to other people for decision-making in an area where the CEO is also well qualified. A helpful metaphor is the simple concept of the driver. If you have a driver, you tell them where you want to go and what time you want to get there. And then typically you let them figure out how to get there, even if you're a better driver. As the leader, you need to know where you want the driver to get to and when you wish to arrive, and maybe you set some ground rules – don't break the speed limit, drive responsibly, and so on. The point where such an approach becomes too weak and too deferential is when you leave it to others to figure out the destination and preferred arrival time.

This approach is described by my former colleague Arjun Mallik, a CEO, as a 'tight-loose-tight' process. It establishes clear and tangible performance targets, allowing considerable autonomy as to the process, but then ensures tight accountability as to whether the objectives have been met.

"The style is sort of tight upfront – very prescriptive as to what the business objectives and deliverables are; loose in the middle, so you guys are responsible and empowered to do what you have got to do; and tight at the end, which is the point of reckoning at the end of the year. The 'tight-loose-tight' phraseology I got from... I think it was an IMD article. It makes the business delivery non-negotiable but empowers the team to exercise their 'ownership'."

The implication for the CEO is that they should retain ultimate decision-making control for strategic and major operational matters, while delegating other operational decisions to those closest to the operational reality with the appropriate level of expertise. As for which decisions fall into which category, this is a question of judgement – a leadership quality typically learned through experience, for which there cannot be a simple handbook or set of rules.

Although some leaders are too indecisive, being too directive and micro-managing is a more common problem. Some executives erroneously think that the reason they were appointed to the top job is so that they can dictate and tell people exactly what they should do, but this approach typically leads to sub-optimal decision-making and weakened employee engagement.

It is worth thinking about the implications of a CEO assuming that they should be the sole decision-maker, over-ruling or micro-managing their direct reports.

- The tacit assumption is that individuals cannot make mature informed decisions as professional adults – in practice, all your staff should be capable of doing this, or you shouldn't have appointed them in the first place.
- If you hire smart people, then act as if they are not, this is likely to backfire and produce sub-optimal outcomes.

A degree of humility is necessary, therefore, for effective delegation.

Yes, the buck does stop with the CEO – all the more reason to be fully informed, engage senior leaders, and get the best out of their talents. Ultimately, most major decisions will be the responsibility of the CEO, but they will be better decisions when the CEO is better informed by their team, and when the individuals responsible for execution are empowered, informed, aligned and engaged.

Optimal alignment

The need for engagement and alignment comes with a health warning. It is a desire commonly expressed by executives, and probably always will be. Given the over-riding need to nurture effective collaboration between functions and within teams towards the strategic goals, and to maintain operational excellence, it is of course a priority. While it would appear to be the case that more alignment is always better, at a certain point it is a quality that needs to be optimised, not uncritically maximised.

The risks that come with high levels of alignment of direction are not obvious when all is functioning well; the products or services are popular, the business is meeting demand, there are opportunities for growth. However, the business's direction may be wrong, or may become wrong, slowly but perceptibly, with the passage of time. Strategies that make sense when established may no longer do so if markets change. Alignment is a weakness if it is accompanied by complacency.

There is an observable trait in some executive teams where they begin to collaborate in an unhealthy way, setting themselves less ambitious targets each year, and in some cases producing flattering reports and financial figures that may disguise faltering performance. In this context, the team benefits from criticism, challenge and exhortation to improve performance. A degree of debate or even discord becomes healthy and necessary.

This presents a challenge for the CEO. How do you ensure that there is enough challenge and robust debate within the executive team to ensure that strategies are properly understood and refined in the light of fair criticism without tolerating so much dissent that it becomes disruptive or even – in the most extreme cases – toxic, with mutually hostile factions developing?

One of the most effective preventative measures is for the CEO to be clear about their expectations of each leader and each function from the earliest possible moment. This ties in with the earlier observation: you can and should delegate many operational decisions, but this is only effective within a clearly articulated strategy and set of priorities, with the lead coming from the top. Another useful practice is to not let a manager stay in post in the same role for too long, as discussed in Chapter 2.

On manoeuvres: The politics of the C-suite

Lack of alignment becomes highly dysfunctional where there are irreconcilable differences over strategy or policy within the leadership team, or where there are others seeking to diminish the current CEO's authority.

If a senior executive is challenging the CEO on a substantial issue, they could be doing it for pragmatic, business-like reasons – there may be grounds for a change in direction, based on data, or other forms of intelligence and business and market analysis. Alternatively, they could have an alternate agenda. Perhaps a combination of these factors is true. The CEO needs to be able to distinguish between these possibilities and separate the issues presented from the possible motives for presenting them. If an individual's ideas have some merit, it makes sense to adopt those that do. This does not weaken the CEO's authority and may even strengthen it, as the CEO is seen to be sufficiently mature to accept a reasoned argument without being knocked substantially off course.

A feature of a CEO that is easy to overlook, or at least underestimate, is that they may be relatively lacking in confidence or otherwise vulnerable. They will typically be highly articulate, but while confident in manner, this can disguise certain insecurities.

Another source of internal tension, and a hazard that is probably becoming more challenging to confront, is proximity bias. Those physically closest to the CEO, for example in terms of meetings, are likely to have more influence, potentially weakening the cohesiveness of the executive team. Whilst some managers with caring responsibilities, or located at a distance from the main office, will often be based at home or otherwise away from the office, others are meeting the CEO for coffee and meetings most days. The CEO needs to compensate for this, building in additional one-to-one meetings for those who are remotely located. Even if these are short and via video, such gestures can be powerful and reassuring. Another potential cause of proximity bias is that the CEO will have to engage with some function heads more than others. It is common, for example, that operations run smoothly for extended periods of time, while personnel issues occur frequently – hence the CEO will be having more conversations with the head of HR than the head of operations. It is sensible to build in additional meetings with the latter to lessen this asymmetry of personal contact.

A CEO is only human and inevitably will enjoy the company of some colleagues more than others. To an extent this is unavoidable; but it is wise to be conscious if choosing to spend significantly more time socialising with some fellow executives than others that this decision will be interpreted politically by the team.

Don't single people out – either for good or bad

Another way to manage effectively through the team, and to diminish potentially harmful effects of internal politics, is to apply a principle that many find counter-intuitive. It is best to avoid singling individuals out in a public forum – which can include an email thread – for either criticism or praise. Public criticism is humiliating for the recipient and is best avoided, even if the failure is considerable. A conscientious individual will already be feeling dreadful while others could be so filled with rage that they begin plotting revenge.

It may seem less obvious to avoid public praise, but this can also prove counterproductive in a less obvious way. To understand why, it helps to view the act from the point of view of other members of the team. *Yes, this individual did well,* they might be thinking – *but so did I! Why is my contribution not being acknowledged?* Praise is often more motivational if it comes from peers than from the boss. A well-designed 360-appraisal scheme can help with this.

Paul Simons argues against forced rankings in performance

appraisals, as it undermines teamwork. "CEOs should stay away from forced ranking because it sets people against each other. That makes it hard for them to work together. It also disincentivises leaders to build high-performing teams – it's easier to have a team with a mix of high and low performers."

Team targets, incentives and shared bonuses can be far more effective. If the ethic of the business is teamwork, it is essential that the reward system supports this and does not incentivise individual rivalry.

Summary

Leading through the team is not a fuzzy case of 'all ideas are equal', or of dissolving a CEO's autonomy or decision-making role. It still involves judgement and individual decision-making – leadership, in short. It involves nuance, some subtlety, but not an abdication of responsibility or accountability. The leadership challenge is to understand and harness the best of the wider team's capabilities, united around a coherent strategy but with some freedom to debate and discuss, with a view to making improvements.

A CEO is more effective when combining consultation and effective delegation than when exercising hyper-control and micromanagement, which are often symptoms of insecurity and fear on the part of the executive. The paradox is that, the more you try to control in a direct personal way, the less effective control you exert. It is better to allocate certain operational decision-making roles to those who know the issues, technology and situation well and are best positioned to make the correct call. Sometimes they will make mistakes. The best safeguards against this are good hiring to all key roles and allowing the freedom to report problems where they occur. The principles of effective hiring and firing, ensuring the 'right people are on the bus', is the subject of the next chapter.

CHAPTER 4
SMART HIRING, SMART FIRING

L eadership through the team can only be effective if you have the right team. This is one of the central disciplines of effective leadership that is obvious to grasp in principle, yet difficult to maintain in practice. The central point of this chapter is to emphasise the importance of getting 'the right people on the bus'. There is probably no more important responsibility. The most effective CEOs are those who surround themselves with brilliant people and are comfortable not being the smartest in the room, ensuring instead that the best people are in the right roles and that they are getting the best out of them. An orchestra will sound off key if just one of the musicians is below standard.

Hiring the right people underpins all the other good practices highlighted in this book: leadership through the team; an open democratic culture; complying with regulatory requirements without being overly bureaucratic; optimal level of engagement; ability to innovate; learning from mistakes; and working back from customers' needs. None of these approaches will be effective with unsuitable hires, and even one or two individuals who are not appropriate for key roles can cause serious dysfunction. Keeping the wrong people, or failing to identify or attract the right ones, can thwart your initiatives and ultimately poison the culture.

However, this core responsibility of the CEO is challenging and takes an emotional toll. A CEO will naturally form quite close working relationships with other senior managers, which means that managing someone out of the organisation who has committed no misconduct can be an emotionally painful process, which some will understandably seek to avoid. The hiring process tends to be more rewarding at an emotional level, yet also fraught with risk, not least because of the natural limits on the amount of knowledge you can have about the capabilities of someone you have not worked with before, which will be the case in most hiring situations.

The rewards of getting the right team in place, however, can be considerable – even transformational. If the strategy is coherent and well understood, and the team is well chosen and aligned, the CEO does not even need to intervene heavily. So long as the objectives are achieved in a responsible and lawful way, the CEO can even offer a certain licence for teams to do things their own way. To take an example from sport: where there is a dynamic, strong team on the field of play and they score a brilliant goal through improvisation, with some players moving out of the positions assigned by the formation, the manager is not going to complain about loss of discipline.

Of course, achieving this harmonious state of affairs at the highest levels of teamwork and collaboration around a shared goal typically requires a considerable amount of foundation-building (see earlier chapters), supplemented by the best hiring and firing decisions.

'Culture' is people

It is often observed that technical skills can be taught, but possessing the right attitude and values can't be, so it makes sense to hire on the basis of personality and values, assuming an essential level of certain skills and capacity and willingness to be trained. There are exceptions to this general principle where technical skill requirements are very high, but even in these cases it would be a serious mistake to overlook the importance of attitude and temperament. An individual with a poor attitude and in possession of scarce skills can be very difficult to manage and may not add value longer term. If someone is not wholeheartedly committed to the company's vision and the strategy, it is rarely possible to turn this situation around, to engage someone who does not wish to be engaged.

Ultimately, an organisation's culture is its people, so it is only possible to build an open, inquiring, team-based and innovative culture with people who are open-minded, inquiring and committed to innovation and collaboration. It is possible to hire for these attributes, using personality-based questionnaires, a thorough consideration of track record, and taking up references.

To a large extent, outside of the extremes of human personality, there is no such thing as a bad employee or a good one. It is more a case of who is right for the role and for the organisational culture, and who is not. Furthermore, the question of cultural fit is context specific. While this book encourages an innovative and open culture, this is not with a view to prescribing the same culture for all businesses. There is more than one type of healthy organisational culture. The category 'innovative and open' is broad, allowing for a variety of organisational styles. And there is a continuum in terms of the degree to which you can be innovative: a start-up creative agency will have more licence to experiment than an industry regulator, so a manager for whom processes and order are important will be better suited to the latter.

The earlier chapters focused on laying the foundations for effective senior leadership: the right meetings; being clear about the strategy and the consequent objectives and responsibilities of the executive team; working through the team; securing optimal alignment and engagement while tolerating debate; and encouraging autonomy. Through these processes, you can identify those who are with the program and those who are not: those whose pushback is legitimate, pointing to advantages of alternative approaches backed with data or evidence; and those whose pushback is more disruptive, because at its roots lie personal ambitions, score settling, or irreconcilable differences. You build up the intelligence that lets you know who in the executive team are most likely to be effective partners. The learning is not all on the side of the CEO; going through this process often enables managers to decide if their future lies with the organisation.

This diagnostic process requires some rigour but should not be too prolonged; a fair judgement can be formed within weeks, rather than months. A toxic individual – someone who is sabotaging the strategic plans, bullying, disruptive, or significantly underperforming – cannot be allowed to remain in post. Some CEOs struggle to achieve their objectives as a result of failing to deal with difficult people as well as challenging issues, letting matters drift.

It can be highly effective to hire someone from a different sector as they often bring unique insights and fresh ideas from outside the industry that you won't come across within the sector. An additional advantage is a defensive one: when such appointees leave, they tend to leave the sector rather than join a competitor.

The centrality of culture is discussed further in Chapter 12.

Firing someone without destroying them

Firing someone generates uncomfortable emotions for most executives. Even those who do not consider themselves particularly sensitive dislike the process. However, it is an essential discipline of the CEO. If you bring in people who fit the culture and the strategy but also retain people who don't, the culture will corrode and you will probably begin losing the right people. Talent attracts talent. An element of discipline is necessary to maintain the culture. For example, if you retain someone who is not performing or not attending important meetings, then this sends an unfortunate signal to the rest of the employee population.

It is essential that firing is done for the good of the business and not to settle scores, that it is carried out professionally, and that where appropriate, the individual being fired is offered assistance with finding a new opportunity. It can come as a revelation to some managers that it is actually possible to fire someone sensitively, and that the person being fired may even thank you in certain circumstances – though typically, sometime later. If the individual is quite clearly in the wrong role, or not suited to the culture or new strategy, there can be a mutual interest in a parting of ways. It has happened that, when an executive has been fired in a sensitive way, they have been rehired later, when at a different stage in the business's development they have become a good fit.

Fairness and honesty are crucial. If a decision to manage someone out is seen to be in the interests of the business and has been handled in a professional and courteous manner, it is likely to be accepted by the employee population. In some cases, the view of the local community is important, and the business needs to avoid being seen to treat employees in a shabby way.

Of course, the gentler phrases for firing someone can be euphemistic: the expression 'letting someone go' implies that they were itching to leave, which is unlikely to be the case, since they might have resigned already. However, sensitive firing is possible in most circumstances. It means enabling people to keep their dignity, helping them to the next step in their career. If you treat people in a shoddy fashion, you can hurt the employer brand, as well as damaging someone's confidence and prospects. As already noted, someone for whom control and order are priorities may be unsuited for a more flexible and innovative culture but may ultimately become an ally if you manage their exit carefully, especially if you help to arrange a suitable opening in a different business.

The benefits of rotation are discussed elsewhere in this book. As well as refreshing the leadership personnel, this is an effective way of signalling to managers that a culture is innovative. In practice, those who wish to stay in the same role for a decade or more are ultimately likely to seek opportunities elsewhere.

Don't pre-announce your promotion and firing plans

Whilst a certain amount of rotation or planned restlessness can encourage an innovative culture, when taken to extremes this can result in excessive levels of insecurity within the managerial population. Overly hasty or unfair firings, and too much rapid change, can create an atmosphere in which individuals constantly fear dismissal, and therefore become cautious and risk averse. Similarly, it doesn't help to pre-announce major decisions on personnel. In one case, as a newly appointed CEO, I mistakenly informed my executive team that there would be no changes to the managerial positions for the first six months of my tenure. Unfortunately, this meant that by the fourth, fifth and six months, the team was increasingly affected by anxiety and performance dipped.

Another learning point from this experience is that six months is too long to establish a leadership team. In Chapter 1, covering the first 100 days, I emphasised the need to get to know your existing team and to understand context and pressing issues before making hasty decisions. However, while this process needs to be thorough, it should not be too prolonged – think weeks, rather than months.

Within weeks, you should have at least an initial idea of who should stay and who should go.

An exception to the rule of moving quickly may apply after managing someone out of a key role. Generally, it is better to have a vacant post than the wrong person in post, and it may be possible for the CEO to be acting head of a department for a time, especially if there are highly capable individuals in the deputy roles.

This option is only feasible if the CEO has sufficient expertise and time, but it can have multiple benefits. It enables managers within the function to act up and gain new experiences, in some cases sufficiently to become candidates for the full-time post. Hiring someone internally is often both effective and efficient. Enabling people to gain additional experiences in this way bolsters a learning culture within the business, showcasing opportunity. If there is an external appointment, then when this permanent head starts they will benefit from a team with strengthened knowledge and confidence. The CEO who is acting head of a function interacts with people within the department in a different way, enhancing these working relationships and deepening their knowledge of the business.

A major reshuffle is better than a succession of announcements

If multiple significant leadership changes are needed, it is generally better to announce them in a single major initiative, rather than on a drip-drip basis. In the latter context, uncertainty and fear can grow as employees do not know if or when the next hiring or firing is being made. Also, with each individual change of personnel, it may be unclear as to the rationale for the change and how it fits with the business's plans.

It is better to organise a major reshuffle, with a clear announcement to all staff. Such a publicly launched initiative offers you the opportunity to tell your narrative and outline plans for the business. With this approach, everyone in the business has a clear understanding not only of the strategy and the plans, but also of the team that will be leading them. With a good hire for each key appointment, the plans will have credibility. It is possible that not everyone in the business will agree with every appointment or plan detail, but they will know where they stand, and the situation will be settled, allowing everyone to proceed in their own role.

A restructure without a change in personnel is unlikely to be effective – an example of the same wine being offered in different bottles. It is usually the case that some changes in personnel are needed for the CEO to ensure that the right team is in place.

Borderline hiring and firing decisions

For many individuals, the incoming CEO's assessment is clear after a few weeks: they will have been deemed right for their roles and the future direction of the company or identified as blockers and managed out. In practice, however, there are often difficult, borderline cases that exist between these two scenarios.

As a general principle, *if in doubt, don't hire, if in doubt, don't fire*. If you are uncertain about hiring someone to a role, better to interview more candidates until you find someone in whom you can place your trust with confidence, avoiding having to manage someone out.

For someone already in post, the assessment will be based on a track record and considerably more information, so a borderline decision that, on balance, they are likely to be adding value will be better informed than for an external candidate. Plus, you will have avoided the disruptive process of dismissal.

Some more ruthless executives may operate on the basis of *"if in doubt, fire"*, but it is worth considering the impact of the loss of that person's contribution: the difficulty of finding someone better; the disruption to staff turnover; and the climate of fear and possible impact on performance that could result from a policy of frequent dismissals of staff with no record of disciplinary problems or significant underperformance.

Useful intelligence on your people

Given that effective hires are some of your most important decisions, it is as important to be well informed in this area as in any aspect of leadership. Informal and anecdotal knowledge accumulated by the CEO about the team will be limited, subjective and affected by power dynamics. That is to say, a direct report will interact in a different way with the CEO than with others in the business, or with customers. It is best to use professionally structured 360-degree appraisals to gather more rounded and objective information on how an individual performs and interacts with others. Such questionnaire-based intelligence can include questions that tease out an individual's fit within the culture.

Risk management is dependent on the right people

When discussing strategic risk, there is a natural focus on establishing and communicating the business's appetite for risk and ensuring the optimal policies and procedures. Such a formal approach is especially important in a regulated sector.

Ultimately, however, the most effective form of risk management is to ensure that the right people are in the key positions, such as operations, distribution and compliance. The best managers and professionals have good judgement and are honest about reporting problems to the CEO. These are valuable attributes, especially in difficult transitions, such as moving towards an innovative culture in a regulated sector.

The calibre of hires is paramount and is a major contributor to achieving and maintaining a healthy culture. As the management thinker Peter Drucker expressed it: "Culture eats strategy for breakfast."

Summary

Putting the right executive leadership team together is a primary responsibility of the CEO. This is one of the key differentiators between those who succeed, those who merely coast along, and those who fail.

Being decisive about key personnel does not necessarily imply being ruthless. It is possible to manage someone out of the organisation sensitively and appropriately, helping them find a suitable new role. The most effective CEOs are those who assemble and motivate the best teams. This never happens by accident.

CHAPTER 5
CONTINUAL LEARNING

When a mature, experienced executive – for example, a CEO – signs up for a training program, the decision can cause raised eyebrows. Questions, sometimes unspoken, hang in the air: do they really need to supplement their knowledge on strategy, marketing, personal leadership skills, or financial analysis? Didn't they cover that in the MBA? Some CEOs decline to take up further formal learning opportunities for fear of giving the impression of being underqualified for the post. It can perhaps be seen as a sign of weakness. A more understandable reason for declining training opportunities may be time constraints, especially if the business is undergoing intense competitive pressure or other demands.

But there may also be a mindset issue. The most confident, or over-confident, leaders may have a tendency to assume that, at the top of their career, they have nothing more to learn. Many executives, perhaps most, will have a coach and some might see their coaching relationship as the only continual professional development they need. Some do not even hire a coach, believing that this also signals weakness.

This book adopts a different view – some might say radically different. At the point of elevation to the C-suite, you may be more in need of supplementary forms of training and development than ever, not least because there is not the same defined program of experience and qualifications compared with, say, becoming a chartered accountant.

The most effective executives adopt the mindset that *I can always improve; there's always a higher level*, compared with the approach of *I'm at the top, my learning is complete and I'm here to guide others*. As with all aspects of leadership, it is advisable to optimise but not exaggerate your humility: it is as important to be aware of both your strengths and areas for development, and not to be reluctant to deploy your knowledge and authority appropriately, whilst staying aware of your limitations.

The world of sport is not exactly analogous to the world of business, but it offers a valuable lesson here: no tennis champion stops training or ceases to work with a coach to improve their game after they have won a Grand Slam title. They will maintain or even intensify their training. Returning to our analogy of the conductor and their orchestra, the conductor will rehearse every bit as intensely once they are established at a major concert hall as during their formative years.

There are few programs geared to the highest executive level, and a coach can often be the most effective choice as a learning resource. Nevertheless, advanced programs do exist. Those CEOs who attend an advanced leadership program will sometimes observe that while the title of the program was about leading in the C-suite, they were one of only a few CEOs attending – the other participants were perhaps functional heads, coaches and consultants. This can even be the case at some of the world's leading universities and business schools, with faculties combining industry experience with academic rigour. The potential for development on such programs can be considerable. For example, they may offer the chance of gaining new insights, learning about new technologies and markets, as well as offering new skills and the opportunity to add significantly to your network, in terms of number, diversity and calibre. If you do meet peers from other companies, they can be a useful source of information and mutual support.

Perhaps even more useful than attending one-off programs is the opportunity for the CEO to develop ongoing relationships with top-level business schools. The CEO can offer case study material and in return access advice from leading experts, provide placements for high-calibre MBA students, and offer the opportunity for collaboration in research programs. For the CEO's employees, being involved in a business school's case study can be hugely encouraging.

Such a close partnership with business schools boosts the employer brand, including helping your company to become regarded as an attractive option for graduating MBA students. This can become a pipeline of recruits to the management team, which in turn may lead to preparing strong internal candidates for promotions to leadership roles, including CEO. Such internal promotions to senior leadership roles are typically a more efficient and effective route than external hiring, as the individual is knowledgeable about the operations and culture. The recruits can see, by the partnership with an educational institute, that the business is committed to keeping a learning environment.

Earlier, I encouraged the policy of rotating managers. If an individual has been in the same role for many years, it helps to boost their learning agility and personal development to be assigned new responsibilities and opportunities, such as leading another function or an inter-disciplinary project team.

Continual learning as a way of building culture

There is a further consideration in continuing your executive education after reaching a CEO post. Far from being a sign of weakness, it suggests to the rest of the managerial population that they belong to an organisation that values learning. The benefits of a learning culture, one that is continually innovative, curious, open-minded and inventive, will be discussed in later chapters. A learning culture can only come about if the people who make up the leadership of the business display the requisite qualities themselves – and that includes the CEO. This fits with the approach discussed in Chapter 3, *Leadership Through the Team*: effective CEOs tend to adopt the approach of always striving to be better and get the best out of the team, rather than appearing to be 'the best' as measured in terms of technical ability or knowledge.

In an economic world dominated by characteristics known by the acronym VUCA (volatile, uncertain, complex, ambiguous), there is increasing tendency to shift the business model towards one that is continually adapting and innovating. This shift is unlikely to occur unless the CEO and others in the C-suite are also committed to continual learning and adaptation. The executive's personal approach needs both to fit the culture and help to shape it.

As an example of a learning culture in action, every CEO, without exception, needs to understand the rapidly developing technology of artificial intelligence (AI), and its multiple and growing uses and misuses. If the CEO publicly pairs with an AI specialist, who may be several years younger, for personal guidance on the potential of AI, this not only better informs the CEO on strategic and tactical choices, but also sends out a signal to the company that its leaders are committed to the organisation staying at the cutting edge of technology. Of at least equal importance is that the learning will be two-way, as the technologist will also learn from an experienced executive about commercial and market realities, helping to ensure that the technology applied by the firm genuinely helps the customer and therefore the business.

As regards a tie-up with business schools, it is common to characterise academics as being at least one step removed from commercial reality and cutting-edge ideas in terms of technology or business models. At times, however, the situation can be the other way around. A business school with close links to top companies can be better informed about some of the most effective practices of high-performing businesses, the evidence base to support the approaches, and the ways in which the newest technology is applied. In addition, as discussed further in Chapters 8 and 9, many well-founded managerial practices have been established for years and are proven to lead to superior performance, but are not universally applied, except by a few leading companies including some with close links to a business school. By contrast, some businesses with no contact with academia may be more likely to fall behind on the latest ideas, and even become out of touch with changes in their own market.

In leadership and management, some matters are in constant flux (technology, the business model, the geopolitical context) and others are timeless (the importance of team building, appropriate delegation, clarity of strategy and information). This observation underlines the value of reverse mentoring and a diverse profile for example in terms of age, professional and cultural backgrounds within learning and operational teams.

Some CEOs do simply manage for the current numbers and for short-term stability, keeping the status quo. If you're running on three legs instead of four you can still get around. They can stop learning. However, this cautious, safety-first approach comes with considerable risk. Most businesses must keep learning and adapting to stay relevant.

Issues of an open, inquiring culture are discussed further in Chapters 8 and 9. This chapter focuses on the personal disciplines of committing to continual learning.

Getting the best out of your coach

For many CEOs, the primary resource for continued learning and development will be a personal coach. The CEO's relationship with their coach can vary. Being CEO can be a lonely experience, so personal contact, feedback and general guidance are valuable, even essential, for many executives. Ideally, the coach should also challenge, encourage, and facilitate superior leadership performance from the CEO.

While the coach may offer personal advice and support, the most effective use of a coach is in learning and development. Ideally, the CEO should look to their personal network for counselling and sympathy, rather than to their coach. A good CEO coach will be challenging, as well as supportive. A most helpful intervention can be in guiding the executive towards a fuller understanding of the most important relationships in their daily role, providing a framework for relationship management and decision-making. A second opinion is often precious when helping to allocate your time. As discussed in Chapter 1, an incoming CEO must often attend to a proverbial 'burning platform' – recovery from a scandal, a failed IT implementation project, a heavily loss-making subsidiary – and there is a risk of this issue taking up nearly all the executive's time, leading to them potentially neglecting some less urgent, but nevertheless important, priorities. Input from a coach can help maintain balanced judgement regarding allocation of time. A good coach will be able to construct a framework for key relationships. They will ask:

- Who are all the important people you need to be aware of in your role?

- How important is each one of them?
- What are their relationships with each other?
- What are their agendas and how do they differ from yours?
- How much do you need to interact with them and on what basis?
- How do you best deal with them?
- What are their personal characteristics – for example, how do they like to receive information?

This seems like common sense, but such considerations are easy to overlook when faced with a busy executive agenda, especially the more subtle points around types of communication. Addressing these issues in a systematic way is a valuable activity, and one in which the support of a coach can be decisive. Such an approach helps identify people who are more important to the CEO than they seemed to be. For example, for a CEO it is sometimes easy to neglect stakeholders, including non-executive board members (perhaps other than the Chair), or the regulator, or the media, or certain internal constituencies, particularly when things are going well. An external expert's observations will offer a valuable added perspective. This can be particularly useful for a CEO working in a culture that is indirect, polite and non-confrontational, where a skilled coach can identify tensions that are not surfaced and share this intelligence with the CEO.

In response to the questions above, a good CEO coach will delve further, asking: *if you are not engaging with certain people, then why*? Is it because you're forgetting, or because you're underestimating their value? Or is there a personal reason why you're uncomfortable engaging with them? Answers to these questions will highlight which personal skills to maintain and address, for example those to do with assertiveness, communication and listening.

Many larger organisations have structured processes in place around feedback and development and a CEO's coach's interventions will be complementary to these. The most common technique is the 360-degree questionnaire. Whether or not this is the formal approach, it is always helpful as part of a program of continual personal development to receive honest and considered feedback on a CEO's performance and presence in the workplace, from team members and other stakeholders. What are you doing right and what are you doing wrong?

When hiring a coach, therefore, the essential elements are to do with the ability to listen, ask the right questions, and guide the CEO towards the best decisions. Recruiting a coach is best done through the business network, taking advice, recommendations and references. The coach is not a counsellor, although they may have training in psychotherapy. Their professional skills as a coach are the most important so it is not essential for them to have also been an executive at a senior level. It is important, however, that they understand the CEO's world sufficiently to know how a board and executive team operates. It is preferable if the CEO's coach is hired and paid by the organisation, not by the individual. The purpose is to enhance performance, and a coach may be inhibited from challenging a CEO when hired directly by the CEO. If the CEO is unsure whether a coach will be effective, it can be worthwhile simply to try out a coach and discontinue if the intervention is not helpful. A common reason for a coach turning out to be ineffective is that the CEO was never really committed to the concept and may have viewed appointing a coach as a token gesture, or something of a status symbol, not requiring considerable personal effort. Any successful coaching relationship requires commitment on both sides.

Much coaching at the executive level is team coaching, which overlaps with the practice of facilitation. There are important considerations regarding confidentiality, especially if the CEO's coach has more than one client in an executive team. There must be clear rules: if any member of a team feels that information they give in confidence is being relayed to the CEO, then trust can collapse, potentially affecting wider morale in the team as well as that of the individual concerned.

A leadership team coach or facilitator can often be effective. As the 'fly on the wall', observing executive and board meetings as a non-participant, they can offer an objective commentary on the quality of discussions and the nature of relationships. In this situation, a high level of professional training and experience is important. For example, an advanced practitioner will be able to detect inter-personal tensions that others may miss. This can help individuals identify issues and separate the personal matters, such as rivalry or dislike, from the professional, such as a genuine disagreement over strategy. This can help ensure a richer quality of discussion on pressing business issues.

The external coach should not replace the proper role of the in-house team. It is the Chair's job, not the external facilitator's to chair the board. A CEO will chair or otherwise direct the executive team, and not outsource this task to a coach or facilitator. On occasion, it may be appropriate for the CEO to ask a facilitator to take over for specific discussions, in cases where the CEO needs to have a significant input. For example, where there is a series of discussions on the company's core purpose, or renewed strategy, this is a subject on which the CEO will likely want to have a strong voice. In such cases, a skilled facilitator might be best positioned to chair the discussions.

Shadowing and reverse mentoring are other approaches that can assist personal development. Shadowing can involve pairing with an executive from a different, non-competing firm and can be an enormously enriching experience. This can result from attending an executive program and working closely with a business school. Your 'shadow' can observe how you conduct yourself in a meeting, make observations on the interventions that went well, and in return you can do the same for them. Such feedback from a peer can be complementary to that from your coach, and from the 360-degree questionnaire.

Summary

Being appointed CEO is the start of a learning and professional experience, not an end goal akin to winning a trophy in sport. The best CEOs, far from seeing learning programs and other experiences as belonging to their past and their youth, will seek to maintain or even enhance their commitment to continual learning. If time pressures mean that attending a program is not possible, a committed CEO will nevertheless continue to read business books and relevant academic articles, and will seek coaching and reverse mentoring opportunities, such as learning about technology from a specialist who may be younger. While it would not be responsible to over-engage in learning activities to the detriment of everyday leadership and operational accountabilities, a strong sense of continual professional development will always enhance performance. Personal development is the individual's responsibility, and it is lifelong. As the golfer Gary Player famously said: "The harder I practise, the luckier I get."

CHAPTER 6
MENTAL AGILITY

Some of the disciplines discussed in this book are well accepted in the educated leadership world but can be exceptionally challenging to implement in practice. Stepping up to the CEO role, which is substantially different from other roles in the senior leadership team, is demanding at least in part because many of the required personal qualities are not intuitively complementary. The ability to empathise allows the CEO to view the world from the point of view of the customer, the employee, the head of a department, the regulator, and so is helpful. Leading through the team – not putting the leader's ego and opinions first – and working back from the customers' needs require a certain intellectual calibre and emotional maturity. So, the required qualities for the CEO role include the ability to empathise, to understand other people's abilities and needs, and work with them, rather than instinctively over-ruling them.

However, these qualities must be combined with the ability to make decisions, including tough decisions, with the commercial interests of the business as the guiding principle, rather than the short-term ambitions of individuals whose points of view you have taken the trouble to understand. So, while you may understand the perspective of a significant stakeholder, you may nonetheless feel professionally constrained to make a decision that goes against their immediate interests – at times significantly so, such as when faced with closing a department, ending a project, or terminating a post (or even hundreds or thousands of posts). As a leader, you must be comfortable with people strongly disagreeing with your plan of action and, in some cases, disliking you for it. Arguably, if you are not encountering any protests, you are not moving fast enough.

Being resolute and apparently ruthless in the pursuit of the organisation's success is not necessarily a power-driven impulse, because it is being done in the interest of the organisation. It is not a selfish drive – quite the reverse as, in making a decision that is genuinely in the business interest, the CEO is prioritising the success of the enterprise over their own interests. Nevertheless, it can still be emotionally challenging.

Each of these emotionally charged considerations is directly linked to an intellectual one: in order to be able to gauge if a decision is in the business's interest, the CEO must be capable of understanding the market situation and the ability of the organisation to meet the challenges and changes required. The commercial context is typically ambiguous, complex, and unpredictable, and there may be more than one course of action that appears viable. Information will never be complete. No one can predict the precise outcomes in advance, or the nature, pattern, or scale of external events that may have an impact.

So, at the personal level there are three challenges:

- *Empathy* – The ability to understand and work through the needs and objectives of different relevant stakeholders.
- *Decisiveness* – The ability to make decisions, including important decisions, in the interests of the business and not necessarily in line with the objectives of the stakeholders the CEO has taken the trouble to understand.
- *Analytical capability* – The intellectual capability to assess whether the business's interests really are being best pursued by a certain course of action. This gives the CEO the foundation to be decisive.

The challenge in combining these three qualities, which are not cognitively or emotionally similar, perhaps explains why a high level of sustained performance by a CEO is so difficult in practice.

It could be argued that the first of these qualities – empathy – is a luxury, and one that comes with a risk of the CEO identifying too much with a certain constituency, causing a distraction from the sober assessments of strategy and related decision-making. The point here is not only that empathy adds an ethical dimension – although it does help with running a responsible business – but that it is an asset in purely commercial terms. Empathy doesn't imply over-identification; it is primarily about understanding. It is a powerful source of business intelligence. If you know what a distributor needs, for example, you are in a better position to understand the extent to which their interests coincide with your own, creating the potential for a new or stronger partnership. Understanding what the customers want should be at the front of every CEO's mind, because meeting their current needs and anticipating their future needs is key to achieving and sustaining the ultimate purpose of any business.

Decisiveness does not imply an absence of empathy. It is possible to make hard decisions that are disliked by those affected in a way that minimises their detrimental impact. For example, see the discussion in Chapter 4 on how you might go about the process of terminating employment.

The CEOs who struggle are often those who focus too much on themselves: their status, achievements, and recognition. It is an understandable weakness, given that achieving an appointment to the CEO role will often have required much ambition, intellectual development, and personal resilience. It is nevertheless a weakness. The reason is that it can result in a skewed priority towards an appearance of achievement rather than towards the strategic best course of action for the business. There is often a *short-term-versus-long-term* consideration in this context. For example, the investment to counter a rising disruptive technology or other competitive threat may be significant, impairing bottom-line results in the shorter term. The strong leader will nevertheless have the discipline to make the necessary investments to ensure the longer-term viability of the business.

Another helpful quality for the CEO is to know the limits of one's own knowledge and ability, as addressed in the previous chapter discussing the discipline of continual learning.

Can empathy be learned?

It is often the case that a successful executive, close to being appointed to the role of CEO, will be stronger in decisiveness and analytical capability than in empathy. So, how to develop one's empathy? It is probably more likely to be the case that empathy can be nurtured and developed, rather than learned, and nurtured through experience rather than a set of courses. One activity that is consistent with the development of this quality is strengthening one's ability to work through the team (see Chapter 3). This provides one of the most valuable learning experiences: by continually seeking to harness the best from the team members reporting to you, you learn to understand others' needs and motivations.

Ultimately, it is imperative that the opinions of all team members are considered and for a CEO to have a deep and clear understanding of their needs and ambitions. Having a coach will often help with this and other learning challenges.

Adaptability and judgement

The three personal qualities discussed above are distinct but complementary. But there is perhaps a fourth, which might be regarded as a feature of analytical ability, and that is *judgement.*

Knowing which quality to bring to the fore requires fine judgement and depends upon context. There will be times when you need to listen carefully to the team or other key partners, because your knowledge is insufficient and they will have valuable intelligence to impart. And there will be other times when it is right to come to a decision because there has been enough discussion, there is little chance of further debate yielding significant additional intelligence, and external pressures mean that a decision cannot be deferred.

Resilience and recovery

It is hardly an original observation that successful leaders display resilience. In particular, they must be capable of absorbing lessons from mistakes, or from a business or project failure, and recover in order to lead successfully again. If you have never made a mistake, or overseen a business initiative or a project that didn't work out as intended, you have probably not yet been adventurous or innovative enough.

While this is easy to understand in principle, the implications for self-management are not always straightforward. Some leaders find it more difficult to overcome an association with a failed initiative than others. The extent to which an initiative was championed by an individual determines the strength of that executive's emotional ownership of the project, and their identification with it. You may have daydreamed about the recognition and accolades that would have flowed from the project's success. The ability to make a business decision to close, curb or alter the direction of an initiative that was not commercially successful is a key strength. At a personal level, this involves nurturing the discipline to step back from emotional immersion in the project, make an objective assessment of its profitability and prospects, and come to a business decision. It is helpful to seek advice, both personal and professional, from your coach, family, close friends and colleagues.

Resilience is also a consideration when dealing with internal politics. Others might be building a constituency that could undermine your strategies. Whilst in role, you should be friendly, caring and approachable without allowing this to impact on your decision-making. Accordingly, some of your most reliable confidants will often be your partner, your coach, and your long-term trusted external friends. It is generally helpful to remember to confide in these individuals and maintain a close network of support, not to take everything on yourself. Many CEOs, including the most successful, are likely to feel uncertain at times, and will therefore benefit from reassurance and support, especially when new to a role or during a period of under-performance, change of strategic direction, or controversy. As the ultimate leader, it is usually wise to convey confidence to stakeholders such as employees and the board, whilst reserving any admissions of self-doubt for your private support network.

There is a link between an innovative mindset and resilience. These are natural partners, because in an innovative culture it is inevitable that not all initiatives will succeed. Failure should be seen as a learning opportunity, and it is helpful to adopt the view that *we either win, or we learn*. To maintain an innovative culture, it is generally better to have seven out of ten projects succeeding, rather than all ten; to lean more towards an inventive and experimental approach, than a cautious one. As with all aspects of leadership, however, it is necessary to optimise. In most sectors, if only one out of every ten projects is succeeding commercially, you will need to curb some activities. Too much failure leads to bankruptcy – you're not building a university of knowledge.

A closely linked attribute of an effective CEO is the ability to stay calm during a crisis. Some individuals almost relish tackling the challenge faced when a disaster strikes, such as a severe weather event, or responding to an internal crisis such as an IT or supply chain failure. The effective CEO does not expect everything to go smoothly all the time. In a crisis, decisiveness and an ability to empathise need to be deployed simultaneously because you must make urgent decisions while rapidly gathering information and understanding the impact, both of the crisis and of your decisions, on stakeholders such as customers, employees and suppliers. Remaining and appearing both concerned and calm is an important contribution. Staff will be looking to you for direction and will gain confidence from the implied assurance that their leader is managing the situation, even if they are not able to control everything. Moods are infectious, so conveying confidence helps to spread it throughout the enterprise.

Can you learn to become more resilient?

All human abilities require elements of both a natural disposition and learned skills. Personal resilience is no different. For some, the ability to stay calm in a crisis and recover from a major setback will come more easily than for others, although these attributes can be learned or nurtured by everyone.

Just as it helps to convey confidence during a crisis, even when you aren't feeling that confidence inside, so it is beneficial to maintain a positive outlook, adopting a *glass-is-half-full* attitude even if the glass only feels about a quarter full at the time. This means looking at the attributes and good fortune you have retained – which might be, for example, good health and a supportive partner. This helps you plot a route forwards. You may have to be patient and work slowly to repair damage and restore reputations.

In the previous chapter, when discussing the role of the executive coach, I emphasised that the role ought to be primarily one of enhanced performance, rather than emotional and personal support for which it is more appropriate to turn to your private network of a life partner, close friends and family. Their support will likely be highly valuable during recovery from a setback at work.

Developing healthy internal conversations helps to keep perspective. There are two extremes to be wary of: on the one hand, there is the insecure individual who will blame themselves for everything and become consumed with remorse which can become disabling; and at the other extreme there is the narcissist, who will always find a scapegoat and never accept accountability. The optimal healthy option involves acknowledging errors by yourself and others, committing to learn from them, and identifying where bad luck and uncontrollable circumstances also played a part. A rigorous approach to such an exercise maximises the opportunities for learning. With this approach, you do not see every setback as a disaster, but you're not in denial either; you acknowledge that things have gone wrong and you immediately begin looking for opportunities to learn and improve. This requires individual discipline, because it can be difficult to devote time to analysing something that went wrong, especially on a project in which you made a significant emotional investment. It's necessary to counter feelings of shame and regret, to stay calm and focus on the facts of what went wrong – or, indeed, what went right, because in many initiatives that do not fully work out, not every feature was poorly planned or executed. Conversely, with successful projects it is equally important to analyse the dynamics, asking such questions as: *why did we succeed overall, or what can we learn from the elements that did not go well?*

Acknowledging mistakes and setbacks with the team and using a setback as a learning opportunity can be the spur to improved performance in the future. In the case of a business's project failure, if you succeed in avoiding excessive personalising of the issues and a blame game, there can be enormous potential for group learning. This is a consideration when hiring; it helps to take positive attitudes into account when recruiting, so that there will be a strong reserve of energy and goodwill when you collectively face problems. This is not just a question of resilience, but of strengthening the learning culture. You nurture resilience by encouraging individuals, including yourself, to continually become better.

Summary

Being a successful CEO does not involve one way of operating, either intellectually or emotionally. You need to bring different strengths and skills to the fore depending on whether you are coaching your team, learning about technologies and markets, or making and communicating major operational or strategic decisions. This requires mental agility: the ability to switch, and the capacity to continually develop the different and apparently contradictory personal qualities necessary for the top role.

CHAPTER 7
RESPONSIBLE AUTHORITY

B eing a CEO does not mean being all-powerful. Previous chapters have emphasised the importance of the limits of influence, working through the team, and functional humility.

However, there is a need for an optimal balance because a CEO does have significant authority, which must be used responsibly and in the best interests of the business. It is as important to understand the extent of your power and influence as its limitations. It is part of your duty to exercise authority and not shrink from making a difficult call. Your decisions will have an impact on thousands of people in the case of a large organisation, or millions in the case of the largest multinationals. They may appear small, such as decisions about the style of meeting for the leadership team; or they may appear major, such as the decision to close or open a division. All these decisions have a direct impact on people's lives. Moreover, the extent and force of this impact cannot always be anticipated in advance.

Tone, as well as content, is highly important in messaging. Your words will be carefully scrutinised and will invariably carry significant influence to listeners, including to small but highly significant audiences such as regulators, politicians and business journalists. It is not only your messages in public statements or group emails that will have real influence, but also the comments you make in internal meetings and informal social settings, including the proverbial chat by the water cooler. It is not always necessary to emphasise your point: you don't have to attract attention. People will be listening anyway, hanging on your every word. Being or appearing to be bullying can be damaging for confidence and morale in the teams reporting to you. It helps to speak politely, to avoid creating fear, but also to speak with confidence founded on a strong understanding of the context and the strategy. It's worthwhile speaking plainly too, providing less temptation and less need for listeners to attempt to decode your message.

Language is not the only type of communication: behaviour also sends a message. For example, as discussed in Chapter 5, a CEO's commitment to starting a mentoring relationship or attending a course of study can give a positive signal, supporting a learning culture. Decisions on who to socialise with should be carefully considered, with an awareness that even your small decisions will be noted and will have an impact.

Part 2, covering the issues of organisational development rather than individual disciplines, discusses how workplace arrangements

that are democratic, with open-plan offices, can be more communicative, collaborative, and high-performing than formal hierarchies.
Before considering a move towards such an arrangement, it is
helpful to consider your own conduct and tone of messaging. A
verbally dictatorial manner in a CEO will have an even more direct
impact on teams that are in close physical proximity. A subtler CEO
will ask questions. Usually, these will be about high-level objectives
– for example, overall progress with major initiatives. However, it
helps to be willing and able to ask about a topic in depth. While the
CEO cannot and should not micro-manage, consistently delving into
operational detail on every specialist area of activity, it's beneficial to
foster an awareness that they are diligent, particularly in areas
where strong governance is essential.

The CEO's whisper: a quiet but influential voice

It is healthy and necessary to encourage and facilitate debate that
may feature strong disagreements. However, these should not be
allowed to become bad-tempered, and the CEO needs to take care
over how strongly they express their own views. The CEO's whisper
is the lion's roar. By arguing too passionately, you could end up
intimidating colleagues and suppressing debate. Your voice is not
equal in weight to that of others.

In many cases, it is appropriate for the CEO to chair a discussion,
especially where others' specialist expertise is highly relevant. For
example, when discussing how a new technology may help the
customer experience, the views of the Chief Technology Officer and
Chief Customer Officer will naturally be influential. A CEO in a
chairing role is often most effective when asking questions, teasing
out issues, and deepening the collective understanding. It helps to
ensure that junior members of staff and newcomers are invited to
give their views, as these can provide highly valuable fresh insights.

Ping Ping Tan, a former colleague of mine and Head of Corporate Communications, recalls the conversations and decisions made

when confronted with a challenging business opportunity. The principle of *Leadership Through the Team* (Chapter 3) and the principle of responsible authority are natural complements, not opposites. She says:

> "Everyone knows [Wilf] is the CEO of the organisation. So, he has accountability for the business and for the team. I don't think anyone felt that his authority was compromised just because he was being very inclusive .... When I say inclusive, in a meeting he was open to listening to different views, different opinions. In fact, he liked it when people gave a different perspective. He liked it when people came up with a creative solution to challenge thinking, and he often asked questions, to get people to think in different and innovative ways."

Such a process helps inform the CEO's decisions but does not replace the decision-making responsibility. The involvement of the team is often imperative both for reaching the conclusion and, perhaps more importantly, for successfully implementing that conclusion.

Dilemmas involving change can call for both in-depth discussion and decisiveness. After having made a decision as CEO, almost all the detail can be left to the team. One significant step is to include the Head of Communications early in a project. This is not as an exercise in 'spin' – quite the opposite, it is to improve the fine-tuning of policy by understanding throughout the course of the project how the policy would be communicated to all affected stakeholders including customers, employees, government, the media, business partners, and the public. Furthermore, by better understanding the potential weaknesses of a decision, they can be addressed before launch. Internal discussion should be both frequent and in-depth: better to have a potentially fatal flaw pointed out pre-launch than by, say, a journalist or a regulator post-launch. Ping Ping Tan, Head of Communications, recalls 'stand-up' team meetings, every day at 9am, during an implementation phase. She says:

> "The daily stand-up meetings were short but intense. Almost every day, someone would bring up something new to the group — a new challenge, a new perspective. Every view was considered. We wanted to make sure we covered all grounds before the launch.
>
> I was involved right from the start, which was really good, because I could understand what the business and government concerns were and what the objections from distributors were.
>
> This helped in developing a solid communications strategy and the right messaging. The narrative was something that was done as a group."

An in-depth, multi-disciplinary engagement serves multiple purposes: to identify and correct policy flaws to convince people of the merits of the policy; and to secure and improve the engagement of all key individuals.

Confidence in both the company and its CEO rises when a bold call is vindicated. This is a rewarding moment for an individual leader, yet it is also a potentially dangerous moment, since they could become over-confident and begin to make bolder and riskier calls. The practice of involving the team, and exercising responsible authority, is timeless and require constant discipline.

Authority in a coaching style

Adopting a coaching style is perfectly consistent with being authoritative. The CEO as coach does not try to direct everything and cannot make every decision. They may appear to be 'hands off' when things are going well, as they see their role as encouraging the creativity and ideas of people in their teams.

In practice – in a healthy, functioning company – talented people will be well qualified and motivated, and will want things to work well and to continually improve. A CEO's wish to be overly directive and controlling is presumably based on an assumption that the team members are looking to avoid their responsibilities and not commit to continual improvement. Adopting an oppressive leadership style with a highly functional team is unnecessary and, of course, will prove to be counterproductive. Letting teams work out for themselves what needs fixing and what else needs to happen, is an empowering experience for them. Members of highly functioning teams hold each other to account. They will possess emotional ownership of the solutions they have devised and will be committed to ensuring the solutions work. The recommended style of leadership in this context is to ask the right questions, ensure that the initiatives support the wider strategy, and let the teams organise themselves. No leader will have a monopoly on good ideas. If you are a recently appointed CEO, you may find that there is latent energy and creativity to be tapped, that individuals felt thwarted by the previous regime and are keen to pursue promising ideas that they did not previously feel authorised to pursue. If you create more opportunities for them, they will be thankful to you as well as hugely motivated.

In contexts where the coaching style is effective in this way, the authority of the CEO is not surrendered, but held in reserve. If a team begins to move in a way that is not supporting the strategy, or even more seriously, if it is conducting itself in an inappropriate way, then the leader must intervene. Being more or less directive is a tactical choice that depends upon the circumstances.

The accidental legacy

The ongoing influence of the CEO can be considerable and will not always be appreciated in advance by the role holder. Some of the things you introduce that you thought were important during your tenure will be rapidly ditched after your departure. Other seemingly less important changes will still be in place years later. Some CEOs find that a major reorganisation, which they considered to be well suited to serve the business for a decade or more, is reversed soon after they move on. By contrast, a quirky innovation such as a different meeting style can be continued by the organisation for decades.

So, be careful what you put in place as a CEO. If you install the wrong thing it could be there forever. It is helpful to be aware of whether a decision is a significant one or not, but sometimes the full impact of a decision cannot be anticipated in advance. A seemingly small matter, such as an individual hire, could have a major impact, while a more substantial change such as a reorganisation may have less influence than you hoped. Indeed, a tendency is to overestimate the impact of structural reorganisations, and to underestimate the consequences of decisions on individual personnel, particularly managers. There can be a belief that the hierarchy, or the reporting lines, constitute the business. In reality, it's the middle managers and their direct reports – how they communicate, make decisions, operate, and execute – that collectively shape how the business performs.

For example, a time-consuming restructure of reporting lines, to centralise for efficiency or devolve for local autonomy, may have negligible impact on market share and other measures of performance; but by contrast, a single personnel decision – such as dismissing a toxic manager who has blocked necessary change – can be transformative, unleashing the innovative potential of the teams. So, while at the start of this chapter it was acknowledged that some decisions are bigger than others, it is essential to qualify this point by underlining that some seemingly 'small' decisions may have a substantial impact, and conversely you may be disappointed with the effects of a seemingly more radical initiative.

Significant improvements in performance can be derived from cultural changes, for example a shift from a rules-based, orderly and cautious culture towards a dynamic, innovative and team-based approach. Cultural shift is challenging, in-depth and sometimes long-term, requiring committed work to engage, inform and empower teams. It may involve difficult decisions in hiring and firing. Structural change is often easier but less impactful, especially if done in an instructional, top-down style. Often, the most impactful change comes from simultaneously addressing both structural and cultural issues – for example, moving from a formal hierarchy to a team-based approach – and it is important for CEOs not to underestimate the cultural dimension.

Not everything can be planned and choreographed in business management; there are always surprising by-products. There will also be unexpected obstacles and challenges – but also, unanticipated opportunities.

Delegating appropriately and selectively

Ultimate executive authority lies with the CEO. You will be held accountable for anything and everything that occurs on your watch. This does not mean that you need to make every significant decision, which is impractical, especially in the largest organisations. This underlines the fundamental importance of getting the right team in place and being confident in their abilities and judgement.

Delegating appropriately is a skill. A function head can often be an effective leader of a particular cross-functional project, and of course the technical advisory leader is the one with relevant expertise. As CEO, avoid over-reaching your authority, for instance by assuming to know more about technology than the Chief Technology Officer (CTO). Don't under-reach either, because the CEO retains overall responsibility for delivery of services and meeting strategic objectives. Typically, for example, a CTO should not have sole decision-making powers over implementation of new technologies, because the ultimate purpose of these technologies is to serve the customers.

The CEO should never carry out a task that is better delegated. It is inappropriate, and an expensive use of your time. Typically, a CEO will have been a functional head in a previous post and they should especially resist the temptation to intervene inappropriately in that specialism, undermining the authority of the present head of function, and being pulled away from their overall executive responsibilities. You can use your expertise in that area to select the best individual to head up the function, and then delegate appropriate authority to that individual. A related problem arises where CEOs set themselves up as a quasi-expert in an area where they do not have a specialist background and assume they can get themselves up to speed with unrealistic haste. Typically, this occurs in areas such as Marketing and HR, which to some are less obviously technical than Finance or Technology, but in which years of specialist experience are equally valuable. Likewise, CEOs with pet areas of particular interest can find themselves in danger of devoting too much time to these.

The CEO needs to have a good overview of all the contributions of the different specialisms, encouraging a highly functioning team where individual specialists contribute in-line with their expertise, having open discussions, acknowledging challenges, and holding each other to account. It is helpful to set up specialist 'steering groups' (a more dynamic term than 'committee') dedicated to certain initiatives, such as new product development or new technology implementation. The CTO will advise on what the technology can do; the Chief Customer Officer (CCO) will advise on how customers are using existing products, what they may like from a new service, and how they would like to access and use it; and the Marketing specialists will advise on how to reach such customers (and so on).

In a healthy, coaching culture, the CEO will often chair such a steering group without the need to be too directive, only ensuring that the projects stay on track. They will need to prevent a situation where a multi-functional project is captured by a particular function. In a technology-led firm, that might be the CTO; in a sales-driven business, it might be the distribution specialists that are encouraging overly risky top-line growth. The CEO can adopt a facilitative role when the team is functioning well, with balanced contributions from all, then make a more direct intervention to correct imbalances that have arisen. It is a more nuanced approach than a top-down dictatorial manner, but it is still an authoritative leadership role. It involves ensuring that no single interest has excessive influence.

Pace of change

Exercising authority responsibly means paying attention to the tone of the message, as well as the content. Another consideration is the pace of change. Previous chapters have referred to this dimension in the context of the first 100 days, and the timing for making changes to the senior leadership team. It is important to be thorough, without being slow. Attending to the correct pace of change is another crucial dimension where the effective CEO needs to strive for an optimal balance. Too slow, and opportunities and momentum will be lost; too fast, and you risk basic errors or not bringing your staff with you.

Making major changes too frequently, without a period of consolidation and adaptation, can result in unproductive turmoil, burnout and confusion. Change initiatives that are frequent, poorly executed or seemingly done for either show or another unconvincing reason – for example, following a fad, or attempting to signal a difference from the previous CEO's approach – will struggle to find acceptance. Employees are typically savvy and can sense if a change initiative is necessary and well thought through. They will quickly become cynical if they feel that a succession of initiatives came and went with little testing for effectiveness for each one – that there has merely been a series of changes for change's sake.

It is wise to only change the things that genuinely need fixing and to carry out assessments on the effectiveness of each project, reorganisation and other initiatives. The one qualification to this advice to 'change only what needs fixing' is to be aware that some ways of working, or products or services, may appear to be doing fine but may still require update, or modernisation, or a similar shake-up. This is where the maxim from management thinker Tom Peters comes in: 'If it ain't broke, break it, or someone else will break it for you.' While it is possible to over-interpret or misinterpret this guidance, it comes into its own where there is a risk of complacency creeping in. There is always the risk of a disruptive technology or an unconventional competitor threatening your product or service, or slowly chipping away at profit margins. Better to anticipate the threat and seek to update or modernise, as part of a culture of continual learning and innovation.

The question of an optimal balance in the pace of change will be addressed in *Chapter 11: Just Maverick Enough*, which explores the dynamics of a well-balanced organisation that can both innovate and deliver.

Asking for direction

It may be natural to assume that direction comes from the top, and that the top of any company is its CEO; in fact, the most senior executive is ultimately accountable to the board, which in turn answers to the shareholders. An incoming CEO is well advised to ask for a clear brief on strategy and operational priorities at the point of interview, as a platform for agreeing a set of objectives for the near and medium term, and beyond. However, the CEO should be prepared for circumstances lacking clear direction from the board.

For example, after the CEO's appointment, the agenda of the board may be heavily influenced by an activist shareholder, demanding a substantial shift in priorities, perhaps towards stronger short-term financial returns or towards a more environmentally sustainable set of policies. Such unexpected interventions can significantly affect the basis on which the CEO was appointed, and the core duties and objectives may need to be reassessed. It is possible for board members to become focused on either tactical or administrative matters at the expense of strategic priorities, emerging competitive threats, or other substantial matters. In such cases, the CEO will need to take the initiative and encourage the co-creation of strategic objectives together with supportive board members.

Everyone in the managerial population should have clear objectives, linked to strategic aims. Without these, it is impossible to gauge progress or have any sense of whether the manager is effective.

Summary

Being a CEO is an active role. There's a difference between an action plan and an action. While CEOs might love to make plans and prepare presentations, staying in the realm of devising strategies is different from getting things done. The role involves management – it involves fixing problems. Often the most effective CEOs solve a problem before the board or other stakeholders in their business know that there's a problem.

This means exercising your authority appropriately. Again, like the conductor of the orchestra, you might not be playing any instruments, but you are making sure the instruments get played, in tune and at the right tempo. You're not letting matters drift, and you're not just making plans.

PART TWO

CHAPTER 8
AN EMPOWERED ORGANISATION: THE OBSTACLES

f you get the culture right, good things will follow. This has been taught by many business leaders over the years, from Peter Drucker to Tom Peters, Lynda Gratton and more. But it also presents us with a puzzle. Despite the evidence base having been established for decades (Jeffrey Pfeffer's *The Human Equation*, for example, was published in 1998), it is still the minority practice to manage through the team to ensure psychological safety and to pursue high performance through engagement.

Professor Pfeffer warned that, despite rigorous studies demonstrating the enormous economic returns to be obtained through implementing what he variously calls high involvement, high performance or high commitment management practices, "trends in actual management practice are, in many instances, moving in a direction exactly opposite to what this growing body of evidence prescribes".[i]

The warning was prescient. A decade later, highly speculative, short-termist practices in the banking sector led to the crisis of 2008 and the austerity that followed. This is just one example of the persistent counter-culture that prioritises management by short-term financial targets and a 'win at all costs' mentality. Even now, the low-engagement workplace is still common. The 2023 Gallup State of the Global Workplace Report found that six in ten employees were psychologically disengaged from work, and that the cumulative cost of this was $8.8 trillion, or 9% of global GDP[ii]. In my experience, insisting on management through the team and prioritising communication and employee engagement often prompts scepticism – although this tends to diminish once the improved results are established.

This chapter discusses likely explanations for the patchy and slow implementation of persuasive findings on the effectiveness of highly engaged workplaces and offers some ideas on how to develop such a culture. It contains advice based on proven approaches in several large and complex businesses on what the CEO can do to improve both organisational culture and commercial achievement. The approach requires discipline, care and thought, but many of the tactics are inexpensive.

Being a CEO involves handling internal politics, the owners' expectations, rapidly evolving technology, and unpredictable markets and geopolitics. It is never going to be an exact science; but that doesn't mean it is safe to ignore empirical evidence and make decisions based on hunches alone. Implementation is nonetheless challenging. While there is a compelling evidence base for the highly engaged culture, you will confront significant obstacles.

Obstacles to the engaged culture may include:

- *High engagement remains counter-cultural* – Knowledge of the evidence base may not be widespread. Some executives are sceptical, or unaware, of the link between engagement and success levels.
- *Correlations are inexact* – While there is evidence and a logical causal link between empowered teams and stronger commercial performance, the links are not always visible to everyone, and there may be a time lag.
- *Unethical practices can be successful* – Exploitative and monopolistic practices can also be highly profitable, where competition and law enforcement are weak. However, organisations deploying such strategies have hidden vulnerabilities.
- *Personal challenge for the CEO* – The personal challenge of being both empowering and decisive, as discussed in Chapter 6, is considerable.
- *Mini-dictators interrupt the flow* – It can happen that a CEO empowers their direct reports, many of whom feel emboldened by the additional autonomy and hold on to their power, rather than further delegate authority to their own direct reports.
- *Internal politics frustrate plans to delegate and empower* – Factional dynamics can undermine well-intentioned efforts to build a participative culture, and team-based initiatives can become discredited.

Discussing each of these obstacles in turn:

High engagement is logical but remains counter-cultural
Effective CEOship is primarily achieved by prioritising looking after your people. It has been popularised in the model demonstrated by Professor Jeffrey Pfeffer in *The Human Equation* and elsewhere and has been patiently built on research evidence.

The approach of focusing primarily on the commercial results and other financial numbers is akin to staring at the compass long enough in the hope that it will move in the right direction. It has been likened to trying to improve your game at tennis by looking at the scoreboard instead of the ball.

Those of us who are schooled in the team-based, participative approach of Professor Pfeffer, or W Edwards Deming and Peter Drucker before him, adopt the philosophy that, if you appoint the best people, look after them and equip them to collaborate in teams, guided by the best strategy, the financial results will take care of themselves. This is logical, because ultimately people are the central resource that creates and deploys all the other resources. It doesn't mean focusing on people solely from a welfare point of view, although wellbeing and psychological safety are important; it means always linking people to strategy, tactics and performance. You figure out what core business outcomes you want, then work back from what the customer needs, and is going to need, and select the right people and teams to achieve this. If you take care of your team, they will take care of the business.

This understanding is logical and supported by evidence, but it is not a universal approach. This leads to an almost comical code of principle among some humanistic business leaders:
'Do the right thing – just don't get caught!'
It continues to be the case that some investments in people and team building appear to be peripheral, self-indulgent, or even 'soft' in the eyes of some board members schooled in the discipline of

understanding business predominantly through the numbers, for example by studying the balance sheet. However, once the good commercial results flow in from investing in teams, and a virtuous circle is established, no one criticises you putting people first.

Correlations are inexact and results may lag

One might think that if the evidence for the high-engagement management style leading to superior business results really were compelling, then the practice would have become universal years ago and the case would not still have to be made. In reality, a commercial organisation operating in unpredictable international markets is an exceptionally complex entity. There are multiple causes, effects and feedback loops.

There may be a time lag between certain investments and the return – the classic short-term / long-term dilemma. Building a team-based culture should not be done too slowly – it is helpful to maintain a momentum, as discussed in earlier chapters – but it does take time. Sometimes, it is combined with difficult decisions over closure or reorganisation of units and some redundancies. For the CEO who wants to build the business, patience is often needed to see a return from investment in people and teams, including where it is lacking in some investors, board members and other stakeholders, who may need convincing on this point.

Some leaders have a very short-term focus, perhaps having made a career decision only to be in a post for two to three years, during which time their priorities are to avoid major risks and longer-term investments whilst ensuring the quarterly results are impressive. Executive incentives can even be heavily skewed towards encouraging a focus on the short-term results. Investors and boards should ideally address this, ensuring that the senior executives are incentivised for investing and innovating – that they are planting acorns every week, not only harvesting oaks. Unfortunately, typical compensation packages reward leaders primarily for the harvesting.

This is especially the case in listed companies, while family-owned firms tend to look to the next generation and are therefore more likely to have a longer-term focus.

Even over the longer term, it may be difficult to demonstrate the links in the virtuous circle of investment in people and enhanced returns. There has been much discussion over the years as to how, or whether, to identify a return on investment in people-led practices such as a management development program or cross-functional teams. If a boost in performance follows, people-related investment might not be recognised as the cause, and it might be thought more likely the result of more directly commercial innovations such as new product developments or changes in the market landscape. However, this would be a partial view, since most sources of competitive advantage are ultimately derived from people, whether they are working in products, marketing, sales or service. You may deploy AI, but the technology, its implementation and its oversight is still ultimately the responsibility of people.

You cannot have an innovative culture without innovative people. You cannot have an ambitious culture without ambitious people. You cannot have an adaptive, agile business without adaptable people. The desire for an evidence-based business case appears rational, but to be consistent this requirement for evidence-based rigour ought to be symmetrical, leading to the question: what are the effects of *not* investing in your people?

Unethical practices can appear to be successful

Some company policies are highly profitable in the short term, but with an approach that is unsustainable, based on misrepresentation, speculation, or even fraud in the most extreme cases. They often result in a corporate collapse and/or scandal; but some people may have earned significant sums along the way, and investors who exited at the right time will have profited.

The issue is complex. In a conventional understanding of the executive's ethical dilemma, it is sometimes supposed that the ruthless, profit-driven, corner-cutting approach is likely to be the most profitable, while a principled approach comes with a cost. While being principled is not a guaranteed route to superior commercial performance and investor returns, it does come with many benefits, some of which may not be obvious.

In strongly regulated countries, an honest and principled company is far less likely to be fined, face special investigations, have to deal with the difficulty of handling a whistleblower, or face challenging questions from the media. A strict policy of being honest and fair, and staying well above the regulatory minimum of acceptable standards, is an effective insurance strategy. In less well-regulated countries, you also receive a dividend. For example, if third parties know you will never pay a bribe, they stop bothering you, saving much management time.

More generally, if you gain a reputation for honest dealing you will reassure your most reliable suppliers, distributors and employees. There is more likely to be an atmosphere of trust, enabling projects to be completed and customers to be satisfied.

By contrast, a business with a culture of 'win at all costs / cheat if you can get away with it' runs the direct risk of attracting fines, disqualification and so on. The indirect risks may be even greater: such a culture is likely to run out of control. As the late management thinker Clayton Christensen wisely observed, "It is easier to stick to your principles 100% of the time than 98% of the time." When a company hits a full-scale financial crisis, it is often the result of an accumulation of excessive risks and rule-breaking that had run unchecked for some time.

There are other circumstances in which organisations with less healthy cultures may continue to operate profitably, though at a sub-par level. Political connections, strategic building of mega-corporations through merger activity, and rent-seeking activities mean that some corporations can have near-monopolies that they can exploit. In this situation, the issue of becoming an employer of choice offers a relatively small additional benefit. They may be 'too big to fail' and are intimidating to regulators.

Such companies, while being sub-optimal in some aspects of employment conditions, can offer high salaries and therefore continue to attract talented people. Although it is possible to operate in this way, such an approach does not harness the best of the firm's talent, and such companies can be vulnerable to a major shock if the competitive or regulatory situation is improved.

The personal challenge for the CEO can be tough

As discussed in Chapter 6, making tough decisions – especially when they are also big decisions, such as closing an entire unit – requires a certain strength. When experiencing feelings of doubt or insecurity, it is likely that a CEO will tend to be more controlling.

Shifting to an empowering culture is difficult, especially if the CEO is inheriting a dysfunctional organisation. There may be preparatory decisions such as removing managers who are bullying or otherwise obstructive. Firing people doesn't come naturally to empowering executives and they may baulk at the implications. Having to manage someone out of the organisation is an unenviable task, and difficult to execute well. The individual may simply be in the wrong role or not fit the company's culture.

Handling difficult or sensitive decisions in a clumsy way can cause factional or other types of negative dynamic to become even worse, so that the culture further deteriorates, undermining any attempts at strengthening teamwork.

One insight to offer on this challenge is that it can help to have a managerial system that is low in symbols of hierarchy. In addition to the benefits for collaboration, such an arrangement makes it far easier to rotate a manager or other individual to a more suitable role without there being a perceived 'loss of face'. The benefits of a team-based, low-hierarchy model are discussed further in Chapter 10, on the open plan office and teamworking. If decisions are seen to be in the best interest of the business they will generally be accepted.

Mini-dictators interrupt the flow

The empowering CEO can encounter a problem in that some managers like to be empowered through delegation of powers from the CEO, but do not wish to empower their own teams and direct reports, instead becoming mini-dictators. This underlines the importance of treating the challenge as an organisation-wide cultural issue, not just a question of delegation supported by general expressions of intent. The CEO should address the issue systemically, addressing all aspects of teams, functions and wider culture (see *Building a system of empowerment and teams*, Chapter 9).

Internal politics frustrate plans to delegate and empower

If factional dynamics take over, the CEO will be wary of threats to his or her position, and often with good reason, so trying to empower teams could be problematic or counterproductive.

There are no guarantees. Although an empowering, ethical workplace can be highly profitable, taking this approach does not guarantee business success. If an attempt to create a team-based culture falters owing to lack of engagement or sabotage, then the whole ethos and approach can become discredited in the eyes of managers, board members and investors.

Summary

Engaging and empowering the people you employ gives you the ultimate competitive advantage. The reasons that prioritising such an approach is not universal are complex – the obstacles discussed in this chapter are real and will be faced by any CEO seeking the highest levels of performance. Fortunately, I was given the opportunity to learn the principles of a highly engaged, high-performing culture early in my career, and was able to put them into practice in successive CEO roles, discovering along the way that they were every bit as effective as purported. It is an approach that works both in theory and in practice. Some ways of achieving this, and overcoming the obstacles, are summarised in the next chapter.

CHAPTER 9
THE EMPOWERED
ORGANISATION: TACTICS
THAT WORK

The discussions in the previous chapter suggest that there are considerable obstacles for a CEO wishing to build a strong culture – one in which there is a virtuous circle comprising high levels of expertise, collaborative teams, high employer-of-choice rankings, and strong engagement, leading to sustainably strong financial performance, which in turn helps to fund continual reinvestment in people, communication and team-work. Many of the approaches recommended in this chapter simultaneously address several of the problems described in Chapter 8. This is a pragmatic book, based on what has consistently worked in practice in multiple environments.

Overcoming obstacles and building a healthy culture is challenging yet perfectly achievable. It does not involve grand gestures and big strategies; some of the most effective techniques are low-key, inexpensive, common-sense initiatives, upheld with daily discipline by the CEO and the rest of the leadership team. This section introduces some examples of these, building on some of the approaches discussed earlier in the book.

First, it helps if you as CEO genuinely believe in the dynamic of the high-engagement, high-performance workplace, as implementing these techniques requires significant personal investment in terms of energy and commitment. While it might also require financial investment for which approval will be needed, supported by a credible business case, not all measures are either complicated or expensive.

Clear the obstacles from the runway

The first thing to do to improve engagement, culture and performance is to remove valid grievances, costs, inconveniences and nuisances that your staff may face. Asking yourself how to motivate your staff is in some ways an illogical starting point; most employees begin in an organisation full of motivation and ambition, but their engagement level tends to dip over time. It drops far less in workplaces with a healthy culture, and in the most outstandingly led organisations, it may even rise.

So, rule number one: before devising strategies to motivate your staff, take the trouble to discover the factors that may be *de*-motivating them, and remove them! This applies particularly to features that are perceived as annoying and are neither adding value nor needed to ensure regulatory compliance.

This may require some time-consuming effort on the part of the

CEO and the rest of the senior leadership team in partnership with the HR team, for example to review employee survey findings, with particular attention to replies to the 'open' questions, that is, the qualitative feedback. For example, you may discover the following:

- There is excessive form-filling or other restrictions preventing a team from taking an initiative that it is qualified to take;
- There may be a manager who is bullying or micro-managing their direct reports;
- There may be an unpleasant physical environment, such as very low or high temperatures, lack of fresh air, or excessive background noise;
- There may be excessive and unrealistic workloads and time pressures;
- Some of the compulsory meetings may be overly long and of little relevance to some invitees.

A helpful metaphor can be the concept of 'clearing the obstacles from the runway' so that the aircraft has the best chance for take-off. One tactical advantage of removing obstacles, rather than introducing an initiative, is that this tends to be inexpensive and easy to implement. If something is deeply and widely disliked, such as too many group emails or unnecessarily long meetings, you can swiftly lift the mood and improve the culture. Productivity is increased for a change that costs almost nothing. I learned of a large executive team in which up to half a day had been known to be spent in a Monday morning executive meeting – *every week*. Some executives would even spend the whole Sunday in preparation. It is hard to see any tangible value arising from such long, frequent and expensive – in terms of executive time – discussions. Many of the agenda issues could be more effectively addressed through shorter discussions in smaller groups, or through written communication, or in some cases could be dispensed with altogether (see **Principles for Effective Meetings**).

Principles for Effective Meetings

Scale – There is generally no need for a meeting to be attended by more than six people, especially a focused, project-related one. As a rule of thumb, if someone is the seventh most relevant person to attend a decision-making meeting on a subject, their time is probably better spent elsewhere, where they are more relevant to the decision-making. The exceptions are for major announcements and discussions at 'town hall' type gatherings. These are, by definition, infrequent.

Duration – Long speeches with rhetorical flourishes may have their place in politics, but not in business. People need to be *briefed* on essential actions, based on accurate and relevant data and supplementary information, then empowered to execute their actions, and subsequently held accountable. Longer discussions may be required for major decisions, especially difficult and major decisions (see below). Being punctual, both on starting and finishing, is efficient but also fair – people know the duration and can plan their day around it.

Decision-making – A meeting is often required to discuss and come to an agreement on a course of action that cannot be left to one individual. It is important to distinguish between a decision-making process and an update, which can often best be done in writing. So, if you are not gathering to debate and come to a decision, do you need to hold the meeting?

Building a system of empowerment and teams

Managers who like to be empowered by the CEO, but do not wish to empower their own teams and direct reports (see Chapter 8), can create a serious issue. Fortunately, it is a problem that can be addressed. It is not enough for the CEO simply to delegate and expect teams to self-organise, and function heads to delegate appropriately in turn. It is necessary to build systems that support collaboration and delegation. CEOs should not micromanage, but should take overall responsibility. They are custodians, responsible for the culture throughout the organisation.

It is helpful for the CEO to create a wider managerial team of around 40 individuals, typically including some from two reporting levels below the CEO – the numbers might be scaled down in the case of small or medium-sized businesses. Although this might generate concern or opposition from the C-suite, it is important to understand that this wider team is not necessarily a decision-making forum, but rather a means of communicating widely within the managerial population. It can foster collaboration between the different functions; creating targets for each team can bolster this arrangement. It counters the effect of internal competitiveness – for example, between functions or certain managers – that can arise because of departments pitching for a greater share of resources.

Of course, managing a large group of 40 or so is a challenge, making it unfeasible for every significant decision to be fully debated. Accordingly, you must be transparent about what the grouping can and cannot do, so that expectations are not unduly raised and people are not left feeling excluded from certain discussions. The meetings would typically be monthly, and the purpose would be for this team to operate as a steering group, ensuring that there is a common understanding of strategic and tactical goals. The team would also help to ensure accountability, as there will be a direct means of communication between the wider management team and the CEO. This will not replace the individual lines of accountability or individual targets; on the contrary, it will help to strengthen such channels of communication by bolstering the wider understanding of the organisation's objectives.

Delegation needs to be optimised. It is good for operational efficiency as well as empowerment to have operational decision-making devolved to teams where appropriate for two reasons. Firstly, the time consumed by involving more senior individuals than required results in higher operating cost. Secondly, the team closest to the issue should be better informed, so will often be better placed to make an operational decision. However, for this to work, the extent of the delegation must be understood on both sides. The priority remains to meet the organisation's objectives, not to implement decisions inconsistent with the strategy. Hence, the lines of accountability and shared sense of direction must be strong.

If a CEO is not involved in a delegated decision, they should not attend the relevant decision-making meeting, as the group would instinctively look to the CEO for a decision or casting vote, undermining the devolution of authority.

Encourage disagreement

A collaborative culture does not mean everyone agreeing with each other all the time. It is necessary and helpful to tolerate respectful disagreement, and to create forums where people can candidly and reasonably challenge each other's ideas, while seeking to keep discussion to the issues and prevent personal hostility. Indeed, it helps to actively encourage debate and challenge, through which ideas can be tested and thereby improved. Management involves choice, and it is valuable to have a deep understanding of the merits of each alternative course of action before settling upon one of them. It is generally healthy to discuss more than one option, as this reminds managers that any course of action is not inevitable. Providing at least one contrasting approach illustrates the benefits and drawbacks of each option.

It is also valuable to have the view of both newcomers and relatively junior members of staff. The best ideas do not always come from the most senior individuals. The CEO needs to defend the right of someone holding an unpopular view to be heard – providing they are advancing a reasonable course of action, sincerely held and with some substance. It can be the case that the lone dissenter is correct and the group is mistaken. Only through open discussion can you discover this.

Measure engagement: qualitatively and quantitatively

An organisational culture can be sustained for long periods, but not indefinitely. Though a culture can be hard to dismantle, it can become corroded through complacency. While a lack of wider awareness of the evidence base on employee engagement does not necessarily imperil the positive dynamics, it can result in a progressive neglect of investment in team building and relationships.

Initiatives to understand employee sentiment are only effective if the data and insights that they generate are intelligently applied to ensure that engagement and performance levels stay high. The fact that you're measuring something is important. It sends out a message; but you have to respond and adapt, as with any type of business intelligence. If you ask employees for feedback on their experience and the feedback is negative or mixed, but then nothing happens to improve or correct the issues being reported, then the impact on morale and engagement is likely to be worse than if you did not measure it at all.

The role of the offsite, facilitated meeting

While the responsibility for creating a team-based culture lies squarely with the CEO, and the organisation and lines of accountability for this cannot be outsourced, there can be considerable value in arranging external facilitation for a strategic meeting. This may be especially valuable if the CEO is beginning a significant culture change, such as moving from a rigid hierarchy towards a more fluid or team-based approach.

At some stage in the proceedings of such a meeting, it can be helpful to ask:

- What are the five or six most important things that need to change in this organisation?
- How do we set about doing this?

A formal hierarchical culture is often a cautious culture, and some businesses might consider the relative benefits of becoming less risk averse. This is especially the case since, according to the World Economic Forum, the inventions of the Fourth Industrial Revolution, such as advanced AI and robotics, mean that business models have shorter shelf lives than previously.

An external facilitator can ask challenging questions that are less likely to result in a defensive response than if they were posed by a direct line manager. Discussions can be more open. The facilitator can ask the CEO's direct reports for information about their requirements and their experience while the CEO is out of the room. The feedback can then be presented openly to the CEO, ensuring an informative, non-confrontational dynamic.

The advantage of being offsite, away from day-to-day distractions, is that you can have time and space to interrogate issues more deeply, and to understand individual ambitions and frustrations. The most effective offsite meetings combine facilitated group sessions with some one-to-one meetings. At such a plenary gathering key principles for ways of working and priorities can be agreed.

Through such meetings, the CEO can become more richly informed of the strengths, weaknesses, and ambitions of key individuals and teams in just two to three days. This creates a foundation of organisational intelligence and shared understanding from which to build the culture. While an offsite, facilitated managerial team gathering may appear to be a 'soft' issue or even an indulgence, it can be extraordinarily efficient if used well.

After the offsite meeting, it is important to maintain the momentum generated. It can be sub-optimal, or even counterproductive, to have an engaging meeting away from the workplace, only for the positive ideas and potential initiatives to be discarded or diluted once everyone is back 'in the office'. It helps to have a follow-up meeting, to hold the executive and the wider team to account and ensure that the promising initiatives are implemented.

Any organisational culture tends to be self-sustaining because of the feedback loops – both the virtuous circle and the vicious circle. In the case of a healthy culture, it is typically unnecessary for all managers in the organisation to analyse the evidence base on the highly empowered, high-performance business for it to be sustained. During a period of success, the business logically continues with all the associated practices. It would be disproportionately time-consuming and expensive to analyse all the causal relationships between good practices, superior attraction and retention of customers, and stronger financial results.

Can an organisation become too engaged?

There is a dynamic that is counter-intuitive: a highly engaged workforce with a strong sense of mission can tip into overwork and collective burnout. Performance may be strong for an extended period and then suddenly dip. Such a phenomenon is sometimes associated with a personality cult around a charismatic leader, who may start out being empowering, but who becomes more demanding and controlling through insecurity or the sheer pressure of the leadership role, or their growing ambition as their personal influence and media profile increases. A leader with a cult-like status and ardent followers is prone to over-reach in their commercial ambitions.

This risk of a personality cult is another reason not to let an executive stay in role too long. After around four years as CEO, you should have a strong following among your teams. With a longer tenure, there is a risk that this bond becomes too close and the organisation could benefit from new perspectives. Most of the initiatives and programs that a CEO can introduce will be realised after four years, by which time it is often healthy to start looking for a new opportunity and to let someone new take over. Presumably, this is one of the reasons why Chinese emperors reportedly allowed their necessarily highly empowered Provincial leaders to stay in role for a term of three years.

It is helpful to keep track of employee engagement levels, for the reasons discussed. Low engagement indicates potential disaffection, negatively affecting customer service and indicating problems with staff retention. The scores should not be too low, but they should not be too high either. Engagement levels that rise about 90% are a sign that the culture is becoming more important than the strategy, and that people are becoming over-committed to work, risking burnout. For short periods, and for a strong purpose – for example preparing for a new product launch or fixing a major problem – it may be appropriate to put in long hours, including some work at evenings and weekends. However, over a prolonged period, this risks personal exhaustion, disillusionment and a crisis in personal lives, such as relationship breakdowns. Work effectiveness can deteriorate, not only because of tiredness, but also because without maintaining healthy balancing interests outside work, one's sense of perspective and judgement can become faulty.

Paul Simons, a Head of HR and former colleague of mine, argues that employees' motivation can be divided into two elements. The first relates to how they are managed, and the second to the sense of purpose in the organisation's goals. The emphasis should be more on the first than the second. Most staff have their strongest sense of passion and purpose around their family and their non-work interests. Many CEOs want to have an impact on the world, and for the enterprises they lead also to have an impact; but it generally doesn't follow that the employees share this close identification with the business's mission. He says:

> "I think that with purpose, we're in danger of overdoing it, because we're assuming that people don't have other ways of finding their purpose. And actually, there is a body of research starting to show that if you're trying to evangelise at work and tell someone 'this is how you find your meaning', they'll reject it, because people will find their meaning through their communities. Many people are looking to work for a company that pays them fairly, treats them with respect, and is in a culture they can be proud to work for."

This does not mean neglecting the concept of an organisational sense of purpose, because people will want to feel that their contribution makes a positive difference. Instead, it means understanding that, for most employees, it is unlikely to be the dominant motivator. The implication is to prioritise the essential disciplines of good management – coaching, informing, empowering, compensating fairly – ahead of inculcating a sense of missionary zeal.

In the most extreme cases of excessive engagement, the leader acquires a near-messianic status. Any disagreement is viewed as disloyalty and becomes political. This is dangerous for any organisation, because no individual is omniscient, and those who believe that they are usually prove themselves to be more prone to error than others. Tolerating and encouraging open debate and disagreement, in addition to helping inform decision-making, helps curb any tendency towards the personality cult. There are other tactics that the CEO can deploy to prevent a healthy followership from becoming an uncritical devotion, and to prevent engagement and alignment becoming excessive fervour. For example:

- If you have keen followers, do not abuse the social power that they give you. Admit when you don't have the answers. Ask for specialist advice, although without ever surrendering executive responsibility for the ultimate decision;

- Find an adviser who does not rely on your patronage, such as a member of the board. They are more likely to give you honest advice;
- Find a mentor from outside the business. This could be from a non-competitor firm or an individual you meet at a development programme. This can be a highly valuable form of support;
- Within the business, try to encourage and respect a healthy work-life balance. Ending meetings on time forms part of this – it is good practice to neither start a meeting before 9am nor finish one after 5pm;
- A useful tactic comes when setting personal objectives for team members. While they will be mostly focused on business outcomes, invite them to share with the team an ambition for their personal life, such as learning a musical instrument. Make this a legitimate subject for the start of a team progress update meeting.

Tone from the top: Ensuring a culture of honesty and fairness

Conduct, rather than statements, tends to convey a message and sustain or erode a culture. If an organisation has a policy of 'zero tolerance' towards ethical misconduct, but a member of staff witnesses an executive discussing the possibility of breaching that policy, then the policy will appear to be purely for public relations, and not relate to actual conduct.

No organisation is perfect, but it is possible, with the right lead from the top, to outlaw the most serious ethical transgressions. It is necessary to instil this discipline at the induction stage, and ideally before the point of recruitment or even application for a role. The policies and expectations should be made clear. New employees want and need to know the culture, the 'way things are done around here', which is supported and communicated more by behaviours than by formal policies. It is not enough to say that you have a pass for 11 months because the annual training took place shortly before your appointment. Employees need to be fully informed no later than day one.

One of the most powerful ways of instilling the code of conduct is to ensure that there are proportionate consequences for breaches in the case of an otherwise outstanding performer. If a poor performer is fired for misconduct, then the popular view may be that they were about to be dismissed anyway. However, if a star performer experiences the same consequence, the message is vividly made that the organisation truly believes in upholding its standards, in all circumstances and even if there is a likely short-term hit to business performance. There is a commercial as well as an ethical dimension to upholding this policy: organisations with a lax approach to standards risk chasing business in unsustainable ways.

It is unnecessary to publicly humiliate someone for failures of the ethical code. However, if someone is dismissed for such breaches, then you can arrange for compulsory training on standards shortly afterwards. This gets the message across.

Summary

The obstacles to a highly engaged, high-performing culture, discussed in the previous chapter, are significant and will be faced by any CEO. Some measures to overcome them are simple to execute and make common sense, while others are more challenging and may require investment and some patience.

Intellectual agility is necessary as there are counter-intuitive insights. Employee engagement should not be maximised, as very high levels bring high risk. Presenteeism and excessive dedication to work can cause performance to dip. Allowing disagreement can help alignment and engagement as it gives space for a deeper understanding of different options and strengthens the decision-making process.

This chapter has introduced some of the proven tactics that the CEO can introduce to instil a high-performing culture. Other helpful features form the subject matter of the following chapters.

CHAPTER 10
HOW AN OPEN PLAN WORKPLACE CAN BOOST ENGAGEMENT

T he previous chapter discusses some of the tactics that can boost collaboration and engagement, with significant benefits for service delivery and innovation. This approach can be strengthened by an open plan workplace arrangement, with practices to suit, in which there are no separate offices for managers, including the most senior executives; people are hot-desking and sitting alongside colleagues from other disciplines, encouraging cross-disciplinary cooperation and teamwork. Working from home or elsewhere is permitted, with accountability centred on outputs such as business performance and project completion, rather than on inputs such as physical attendance.

This type of working environment is best implemented by taking a holistic approach, from addressing behavioural matters such as the conduct of senior executives, to the layout of the office floor itself and determining which facilities are really needed and which can be done without. A visitor to the office will encounter a scene rather like a large coffee shop, with people sat at clusters of desks, working and holding conversations, with some private meeting rooms off to the side. It is not possible to discern, just from appearance or location, people's status or specialisms.

This chapter addresses the organisation of a large service industry office, but the same principles of teamwork and close collaboration can be applied to manufacturing. Since the early 2020s, a higher degree of working from home has been the norm, resulting in hybrid operations. The principles in this chapter still apply to the hybrid workplace. To a large extent, 'open plan' is more of a mindset than a physical layout, guided by objectives and focused on teams, with reduced visible symbols of hierarchy. In the early 2000s, this way of working was rare, and considered by some as radical; by the 2020s it was less so as home working had already become acceptable.

For many businesses, including some of the most highly engaged and high-performing organisations, the open plan office is the norm, and those enjoying the benefits see no advantage in reverting to the stifling siloed culture where finance is on one floor, HR on another, and perhaps the senior executives have their own private offices next to a boardroom on the top floor, with thicker carpets, better quality coffee and pastries, and so on.

Objections and challenges, and how to deal with them

For many individuals, especially senior managers and those

raised in a formal culture, the open plan office is a radical culture shock, and may be unwelcome and resisted. A CEO wishing to introduce such a change may encounter many objections, some of which are frivolous or linked to the vanity of a manager. Others have more substance, but pragmatic arrangements can overcome the issues raised.

Confidentiality

You will hear that private offices are essential for confidential matters such as discussing market-sensitive information, or holding a telephone conversation in which a colleague's or a customer's private information may be relevant. This is an important consideration, yet it is not really an obstacle, provided individuals are well trained in matters of discretion and privacy, and that there is sufficient provision of separate meeting rooms for all staff, where private conversations can be held. The point of confidentiality is often raised by the small proportion of managers who in previous arrangements had their own offices – in which case a reasonable question can be put to them: is confidentiality not likely to be an issue for all employees, not just for managers?

Resourcing

A common reaction is: *will I have nowhere to sit if we're all hot-desking and everyone decides to be in the office at the same time?* Resourcing must be adequate. If there are insufficient desks, or meeting rooms, this must be addressed.

'It doesn't fit with the culture of this country / company'

While it's paramount that a nation or other geographic region or company's unique culture must be respected, there is a universality to humankind, and one of the common features is the enhanced level of performance that is derived from teamwork. High levels of collaboration are invariably beneficial, provided that the approach is well executed and supported. This approach has been highly effective, including in long-established businesses in mature, regulated industries in countries where hierarchy has traditionally been valued. The open plan office may be more associated in many people's minds with a hi-tech company, rather than an established business, but in practice there aren't any 'no-go' areas for this more democratic and inclusive approach to organisational management.

Fear of loss of status and managerial authority

Some senior managers worry that their status and authority will be diminished should they sit alongside other staff at a cluster of desks in the main office, rather than in their own space. In practice, this fear is rarely realised. Indeed, the situation is rather the reverse: the physical trappings of status might mask insecurity and lack of true leadership authority. If you cannot establish your credibility as a leader of people and of a business through your own conduct and decision-making, then you will struggle in many aspects of business leadership, especially harnessing the engagement of the teams that report to you. It is important, however, not to surrender your authority as a senior leader by avoiding important decisions or acting as just one of the team members. In practice, employees respect the authority of the role of the CEO and will defer to you for decisions. You are approachable and still in charge. It is a myth that remoteness in business leadership enhances authority and respect.

Principal advantages of the open plan approach

When the open plan approach is well implemented it can enhance, even transform, a business's culture. Each benefit – better communication, collaboration, ability to be well-informed, enhanced decision-making – tends to support each other. The principal benefits are discussed below.

Greater collaboration

This is one of the most valuable assets. The ambition of many business planners to foster strong cross-disciplinary collaboration can often be held back by an unsupportive office layout. It helps to have a policy of mixing and rotation, so that all the finance people, for example, are dispersed among colleagues rather than clustered at one end of the office.

It is necessary to assign everyone their own personal locker, as they will probably not have a set of personal drawers next to a hot-desk; and people will naturally sit quite close to their locker. Instead of clustering the lockers together by professional specialism, you can select another 'random' method, for example, by month of birth, in which case, all the September-born people from different functions, will have the opportunity to be close to each other.

An arrangement that works well is to locate all Personal Assistants (PAs) in the same cluster – these individuals and any receptionists may indeed be the only ones to have their own desks. There are many issues on which PAs need to collaborate, and it is more effective than each PA being in a different area, perhaps traditionally within their own department.

Sometimes, professionals of the same discipline will need to work in close proximity as a functional team such as when marketing specialists are working on a new advertising campaign or technical specialists enhancing cyber-security. For their functional team meetings, they can book a room. Of course, these days many such meetings are held via video link. Moreover, even in quite specialist projects, it is often useful to have some representatives of different functions, so that the solutions devised are informed by different points of view, such as that of the customer or the supplier.

Managers are more approachable

If a hierarchical system is in place, and especially if it is reinforced by multiple points of physical architecture – including a large private office 'guarded' by a PA – there can be a powerful sense of fear among the rest of the staff, akin to the sensation of standing outside the school headteacher's office.

While a degree of respect for authority is necessary, actual fear is likely to be corrosive to culture. The fear of giving bad news to the boss ironically weakens their actual authority by keeping them in ignorance of the real situation. It inhibits or prevents a coaching style of leadership in which those with experience can bring the best out of the people less senior than themselves. In a culture where leaders are accessible and approachable, they can offer the benefit of their experience to their teams, enriching the organisation's knowledge and capability.

It is true that, in certain situations such as a crisis, a leader must be directive. Fortunately, these moments are relatively few, and in such cases the context creates a sense of urgency so that people are looking to the leader for decisiveness. Most of the time, the leader's appropriate role is one of guiding and team building. Generally, your staff will want to succeed and do well, and your job is to help them do that, whether by achieving your customers' desired outcomes or by delivering your organisation's strategic goals.

To ensure these benefits, it is necessary for leaders to be temperamentally as well as physically approachable. It does not help the culture if, having reorganised the workplace to be more open and democratic, leaders scowl every time they are asked for advice, or act in a patronising or dismissive manner. While there are times when you cannot be immediately available upon request, all matters should be dealt with in a courteous and professional manner. The open culture is behavioural as well as structural.

Managers are better informed

One of the most time-wasting practices in conventional management is the writing of frequent and lengthy internal reports. To a degree, this is a symptom of physical separation between senior executives and their teams: because they cannot observe or experience what is going on in operations, they desire to be briefed in a formal manner. This embodies elements of the vicious circle: the more time is taken up with reading reports and discussing the implications in the executive suite, the less time there is for visiting the 'shop floor'. As a result, more written intelligence has to be delivered to the executive team.

When the senior managers physically inhabit the same location as the other staff, they can observe much for themselves and can ask questions directly of key personnel over lunch or by the watercooler – a much more efficient and effective form of communication than formal reporting, with the additional benefit of aiding the bonding and teamwork that help organisations deliver. Moreover, managers will observe and experience the real culture – those intangible but essential features that reflect the energy and commitment of the employee population.

Faster decision making

Constant, real-time intelligence gathering by decision-makers within the business informs decision making that is faster and likely to be better. The CEO and the senior team can spend less time reading long reports by market researchers or the head of IT before making an important decision, such as how to deploy AI in service delivery, because they have been holding frequent conversations with the appropriate members of their team on the matter for weeks on an almost daily basis.

However, there does need to be some formality in decision-making and accountability. The approach described in this chapter is not structureless. It is fluid and adaptable, but there is a structure to the teamwork. This is discussed in *Chapter 3: Leading through the Team*.

Watercooler conversations and a greater 'buzz'

This approachability between senior executives and staff, and across teams and disciplines, helps engender a positive culture, a sense that everyone is committed to helping the customer, seeking new solutions, and pursuing strategic objectives. The preponderance of informal conversations enhances social bonding, and such chats often lead to creative ideas.

This dynamic must be balanced with the need for a degree of remote working in the interests of flexibility; inclusion for those with caring responsibilities; and a healthy work-life balance. In practice, an effective policy is to adopt a hybrid approach, seeking the best of both worlds with some presence in the main workplace encouraged.

Enhanced efficiency

The direct cost savings of an open plan workplace can be significant. A more democratic arrangement takes up less space. You may have a cluster of six desks in the space that had previously been occupied by the office of a single manager, while the dividing walls themselves take up space that ultimately must be paid for.

The best open plan office is a paperless office. One organisation planning to implement an open environment removed all waste-*paper* bins as a symbolic first step. For such a seemingly modest initiative, this caused a remarkable degree of comment and consternation! The underlying principle was that, wherever possible, written communication should be digital rather than paper-based. After a period of adjustment, it worked well; it involved a behavioural change akin to the culture changes we have observed, but eventually everyone adapted.

For regulatory and other purposes, some types of written documentation must be stored for a defined number of years. This can be done securely on a storage site, typically outside the city centre where land and property costs are lower, rather than in filing cabinets in the office. This results in further removal of wasted cost, perhaps to be utilised for value-creating endeavours.

Reduced insecurity and an end to petty jealousies

As discussed previously, the provision of a private office is no substitute for genuine leadership authority. By removing such perks, the true calibre of the manager is exposed. In the open plan office, petty concerns over status are dispensed with completely. It has been known in a hierarchical structure for managers to complain if their office is smaller than someone's of similar rank, or further away from the CEO's office, or lacking in certain amenities. All such concerns relate only to the vanity of the individual – they have nothing to do with the performance of the business.

As with high-engagement culture generally, once the benefits of the higher levels of collaboration and team-working are felt throughout the organisation, including by shareholders, there is little or no significant opposition. In one example, following such an implementation, the CEO's successor sought to reverse the reforms and proposed to senior managers that they should each have their own office. Yet the managers resisted and successfully opposed the reversal, supported by the rest of the employees. They did not wish to end the open office practices they were now so comfortable with, through which they and the business were thriving. They wanted to stick with the lower symbols of hierarchy and the freedom to meet with and work alongside others throughout the business; they did not wish to be confined again to their own silos or cells.

Execution is everything

The principal obstacle to effective operation of the open plan workplace is poor implementation. It should be an obvious point, but moving to an open plan office must be well planned, well communicated and well executed, supported by the right behaviours. Poor execution is a more common explanation for project failure than poor conception – this is true of most business projects.

It shouldn't be rushed. If people come into the office one Monday morning to find their office gone and people from another function sitting near them, the sense of loss and disorientation will be considerable. It is appropriate to prepare thoroughly and to communicate well, to listen and treat people with respect. Some concerns around open plan working areas are trivial or self-serving, but others are not. Confidentiality, as discussed, is important, and you must reassure people that it can and will be dealt with. There may be concerns over lack of access to desks or other facilities, so the provision of resources must be adequate.

The plan and the principles underlying the open plan office must be consistently upheld, including by the most senior executives. It has been known for some CEOs to devise democratic offices with hot-desking for staff and other managers, while awarding themselves a palatial private suite on the top floor. This is invariably worse than not engaging with the approach at all.

Some people just dislike an open culture so much that a compromise cannot be achieved and the conclusion is that the individual is better suited elsewhere. For this reason, it is vitally important to be honest about the working arrangements well before the point of hiring, especially in the case of senior managers who might expect their own private office and other such trappings of status.

Summary

The open plan office needs to be carefully planned, well executed, and supported by the right conduct and values, especially on the part of senior executives, including the CEO. The advantages are numerous, including the potential to rescue a business or set it on the trajectory to higher levels of innovation and other aspects of added value. It frees up resources, thinking, time, and energy. You will simply get more done.

CHAPTER 11
JUST MAVERICK ENOUGH

O ne feature where the optimisation of a leader's attributes is of central importance is the degree to which you balance disruption and order. If a well-established business is to avoid complacency and stagnation, then original thinking and experimentation are essential. This should be obvious, just as it should be obvious that capacity to innovate is always needed, or that too much simultaneous radical change can disrupt service to customers, or risk regulatory breaches. However, in practice it can be temperamentally, intellectually and operationally challenging to find the optimal balance.

Much depends on the business phase. A long-established firm with significant but declining market share will, at the very least, require a degree of shaking up, and probably quite radical change, while a startup that is understaffed and growing rapidly will require the introduction of new processes and rigour. Many businesses are at neither end of the spectrum – they are neither a chaotic startup nor a stagnant giant – so the leader needs to possess strong analytical skills and judgement regarding the business phase, and the ability to oversee an optimal level of change and adaptability.

The ability to innovate is essential for all businesses in all phases of development, and at all points on the orderly-versus-chaotic spectrum. Creating a culture of continual learning and adaptation is the ultimate enabler for change, whether that is radical upheaval or more moderate reform. As discussed in the previous chapter, various features may be combined: moving from a traditional office layout to an open plan space; supporting teamwork; encouraging collaboration and collective learning.

The challenge is also considerable when introducing an element of order to a startup. For example, there may be inadequate or inconsistent vetting arrangements for new staff (including for critical roles), insufficient financial reporting, or an inefficient supply chain. Such disciplines, requiring a strong element of order and predictability, may be considered dull by some company founders. Throughout the history of business, a common and effective model for a working partnership has featured a maverick inventor working closely with an experienced business partner who is schooled in operational and financial discipline.

The personal challenge and the organisational challenge

In terms of personal temperament, it is necessary to seek a balance between a disposition towards change, and one that favours stability. At an organisational level, the key to finding an optimal balance lies in the policies and practices described in earlier chapters. In other words, as CEO, you don't prescribe an optimal level for the pace of change; rather, you put in place the teamwork and discipline of continual learning so that the teams will be able to figure out the appropriate pace themselves and discover the changes that are effective.

Strategy-setting is not devolved, but much of the operational detail is, including the degree of innovation and the pace of change. It is similar with creativity: it doesn't work for a CEO to urge people to be more creative, to treat creativity as an input from above; rather, it should emerge naturally from an open-minded, collaborative culture. Most people are inherently creative, and at least part of your role as CEO is removing the obstacles in the way of responsible creativity and innovation. However, the CEO still has a leading role, and not a passive one. If you see too much caution, or too much reckless experimentation, it is necessary to intervene, perhaps using your experience to guide the team.

Paul Simons recommends defining broad objectives for a team and ensuring that each member has a contribution to make towards achieving the team's goals, saying, "If you want to kill innovation, put an incentive plan behind it".

This insight draws on the research, by the thinker Alfie Kohn and others in the field of cognitive psychology. In his ground-breaking work published in 1993 *Punished by Rewards*[i], Kohn explained how the simplistic thinking of 'Pay this and you'll get that' rarely works and often delivers the opposite of the policy intention. Financial incentives tend to have unexpected consequences and might even be interpreted as insulting or demeaning such as conveying the tacit message to research scientists that they do not wish to uncover new findings and must be bribed into doing so.

At the organisational level, an enterprise that has outstanding functional leaders in key roles, a high degree of collaborative ability, and strong accountability and performance management, will tend to be innovative and adaptable. The discussion about open plan offices in the previous chapter might not appear closely related to the subject of this chapter, but in fact, the issues are germane. An open plan office is a means to an end, encouraging and facilitating cross-disciplinary collaboration, simplifying and strengthening lines of communication between the market and the teams, and between the teams and the leaders. All specialists – tech people, compliance officers, distribution specialists, marketing, supply, HR and others – are committed to serving the customer more effectively or discovering new markets and other new opportunities. In such a culture, the business is likely to be collectively 'just maverick enough'.

While the leader and the wider organisation should be continually disposed to change, you should also have the patience to wait and see if an innovation is working. It doesn't help to be continually tinkering. A significant innovation or other change is best implemented as a major project, then left to proceed for a while as you gauge the impact. In the meantime, you can develop another innovative initiative.

Staying onside – the art of innovating responsibly and legally
Given the importance of introducing structure and systems to a fast-growing young company as it scales, there is an irony: as an executive you can often enjoy as much freedom to experiment and innovate in a long-established firm as in a younger one. In an established, mature business, the guardrails are already in place; not just through the presence of a capable compliance function, but more generally throughout the employee population, featuring a culture both of knowing what the regulations are and of disciplined commitment to obeying them – and in the healthiest cultures going beyond the regulatory minimum and upholding high ethical standards. Even the most charismatic CEO would not be permitted to breach the written rules, or even many of the unwritten ones. For a CEO committed to innovation in such a situation, however, there

can be a remarkable degree of freedom whilst staying within the limits, regarding ingenious use of technology and improved service to seek out new markets or improve value for money for existing customers. Paradoxically, institutional curtailment of freedom can be liberating.

By contrast, at a startup – especially in a heavily regulated sector – the most appropriate opening line of an incoming CEO may well be: 'My priority is to keep you out of jail.' In many jurisdictions, regulation is strong, with common themes in different regions. There can be strict rules covering conflicts of interest, limits on compensation, and so on. Moreover, the industry regulator's primary objective might be one of safeguarding the consumers' interests, as there may not be a separate consumer rights body. There may be more restrictions on pricing and product features in certain countries; these may be particularly strict because the regulator has limited resources and can only monitor a limited range of offerings. Another essential discipline for all jurisdictions is continual monitoring of the regulatory framework, as the rules may be subject to frequent change.

The leader's ability to display empathy, as discussed in earlier chapters, is not only relevant to customers, suppliers and internal relationships; it can help with more formal stakeholders. For example, it might help you understand the agendas of the country's governing party, regulator and other government agencies. Typically, regulators want to prevent business collapses and mis-selling, or other forms of wrongdoing affecting customers. International reputation is a major consideration. A government will want their nation to have a reputation for integrity and fairness, one that offers a safe place for investors. Even a small firm going under will be of concern, as there may be ripple effects through the industry. These principles hold in all regulated industries, such as pharmaceuticals, oil and gas, financial services and so on.

If, as CEO, you take the trouble to understand the regulators' perspective and objectives, this will help you in your dealings with them. Typically, they are risk averse and want to know what's going on in the market, while wishing to preserve a sound international reputation. If you establish a good working relationship, based on respect and an appreciation of their agenda, this will be to your advantage.

Some regulators welcome a degree of innovation within their business sector, as part of a policy of encouraging business development and inward investment, provided it is responsible. In a similar way, an effective internal compliance team will not necessarily be anti-innovation. They want reassurance that the letter and the spirit of the law are being adhered to. In fact, it has been known for a compliance team to be just as proud of winning an award for innovation as those directly involved in designing the new products. Innovation is the art of the possible and applies to all.

While many of these observations relate to a regulated industry – with an identifiable institution overseeing statutory rules specifically for the sector, and often possessing quasi-judicial powers – it would be a mistake to believe that there is such a thing as a completely unregulated area of economic activity. This is the salutary lesson learned by some of the cryptocurrency firms that were affected by collapse and scandal in the early 2020s. Whilst there was no specified institution regulating the cryptocurrency sector, or no set of laws governing their manufacture and distribution, what some of the more speculative entrepreneurs discovered was that they were still covered by rules concerning auditing regulations and fraud prevention[ii].

What is maverick?

Sometimes, a maverick point of view becomes mainstream, as the evidence base for it grows and becomes unanswerable. Many of the practices described in this book have been considered 'maverick' by some business managers, especially those schooled in the discipline of just managing the numbers. However, the approach of managing through the team and seeking high engagement is more rigorously evidence-based than many alternative approaches to business management. It is based on applying the timeless ideas of leading thinkers such as Tom Peters, Jeffrey Pfeffer, Peter Drucker and others, and on the research that underpinned them.

As discussed in Chapters 8 and 9, some of these ideas have been slow to reach the mainstream and implementation has been patchy. Some of the reasons for the uneven progress are understandable, others less so. Those businesses that implement them conscientiously and consistently tend to strongly outperform others, including on financial metrics and especially when measured over the longer term.

So, a healthy discipline for all managers is to be rigorous when confronted with an alternative approach, or a new idea. It may appear to be maverick, or untested – but is it really? Ask yourself, 'What are the facts? What is the evidence? What are the opportunities and drawbacks?' Be symmetrical in your inquiry: interrogate the rationale and evidence for the proposed new way of working, and apply the same rigour to existing, established approaches too, because they may have been adopted through convenience and custom, rather than on the basis of a rational case.

A tip for sustaining an innovative culture, and for avoiding the trap of continuing a legacy way of working that is sub-optimal, is to invite observations from new staff, including junior staff. You may need to hire people who will challenge the culture, rather than simply adopt it. Give everyone a say. A newcomer, before they adapt, may have a particularly astute observation regarding a cultural quirk or idiosyncrasy, and be able to offer a considered view on whether the practice adds value or not.

The individual challenge

Personal resilience when an initiative fails, including a willingness to acknowledge errors and rectify them, is an essential quality for an executive. It can take courage to experiment, especially with a radically different approach in an established firm, such as the open plan office featured in the previous chapter. The first part of this book covers many of the personal qualities that are necessary in developing and maintaining your personal resilience and adaptability – in particular, functional humility, the ability to delegate, and commitment to continual learning.

Continual collective learning and resilience

The discipline of continual learning is vital for the organisation, not just its leader. Be prepared to experiment and discover as you go, remembering that you're not in the cartography business – that is to say, it is usually inefficient and unhelpful to spend an overly long time preparing a precise implementation map following analysis of a business situation; sometimes, it's better to just get moving. 'Any old map will do' at the start, but – and this is an important but – you gather factual details and refine the map as you go along.

Capacity to change is best nurtured as a collective discipline. As with creativity, it cannot be decreed by the CEO. Rather, the senior executives should encourage it through key decisions, by displaying tolerance, and by setting healthy precedents. You cannot simply ask people to be resilient: you must create an environment that encourages resilience, so that people will bounce back. No individual is infinitely resilient, and most people will thrive in a healthy culture and suffer stress in an unhealthy one.

Key to encouraging collective resilience is how you react when your teams have tried something that didn't work out. Provided they have been conscientious, professional and have operated within the culture and established rules, they should be rewarded – even if the new venture failed. Leaders should not be hypocritical, making excuses for their own mistakes whilst severely punishing others. Moreover, the word 'mistake' is not an accurate term for an initiative that did not work out, providing there were strong prospects of success at the outset. It's worthwhile adopting the mindset that 'if every initiative succeeds, we are not being innovative enough'.

One approach that has been effective is to have an 'awards night' for learning experiences, with a focus on unsuccessful initiatives. This may include 'failures' (or, more euphemistically, 'unexpected moments'), but will more typically recognise innovations that didn't work out as intended. For the inaugural awards event, you might invite only senior individuals to collect the awards, so as not to embarrass relatively junior individuals, and the recipient leaders would then be invited to share what they have learned from the experience. This is another tactic that helps build a culture of learning, innovation and resilience.

The concept of continual learning and adaptation can be a more helpful framing than commitment to change as an end in itself. An optimal propensity for change means being prepared to amend or cancel a new initiative. Just as it is possible to be overly emotionally attached to an established way of working that is failing or sub-optimal, so it is also possible to be excessively committed to an innovation that is unsuccessful and likely to remain so. There must be credible prospects and sound reasoning for continuing, or the business will become prey to fads or irrational exuberance.

Part of the art of being innovative is knowing what to maintain. In an established company, a feature that typically needs to be left unchanged is the logo. A different design, even a slightly different colour, can be off-putting to customers who place trust in the brand. A changed logo could, for example, even appear to belong to a counterfeit operation, or in some other way weaken trust, with no compensatory gain for the business.

On the other hand, some areas that appear to be so well established that they cannot be altered can be surprisingly fertile ground for experimentation and improvement. One such area is distributor remuneration systems. I recall a case in which, following a discussion with an executive from the cosmetics industry who paid tens of thousands of sales agents on a daily basis, there followed an initiative to introduce the same in insurance for agents, for which monthly payment had been the norm for decades. This prompted a great deal of scepticism and questioning within the company, with warnings of a higher and more complicated administrative load and excessive establishment costs. As it turned out, the implementation was remarkably straightforward. It was hugely motivational for the agents and it improved cash flow for the business as the agents started booking their sales also on a daily (rather than month-end) basis, and therefore faster for customers too.

Summary

Change is inevitable, and innovation is a must. A healthy culture experiments and learns from experience, hard facts and evidence, not from rumour or popularity of fads. There is collective resilience and capacity to learn and grow, helped by the tactics described in this chapter.

A different way of thinking or operating can often be liberating and profitable – and not always the huge challenge it seems at the conceptual stage. What appears to be a cultural change often is not; what appears to be difficult to implement may be straightforward; and what appears to raise problems for a regulator may be neutral, or even positive from a regulatory point of view. A maverick may be a fool or a genius. Until you investigate, discuss, explore and experiment, you cannot know.

The ultimate test of whether change has worked is whether it delivers better value for customers, in turn helping the organisation. Understanding the customer's perspective, and working back from their needs, or innovating to anticipate new needs, is still not universal practice in business. This will be the subject of the next chapter.

CHAPTER 12
WORKING BACK FROM THE CUSTOMER'S NEEDS

On a single day, within just an hour or so, I experienced contrasting approaches to customer service. Returning a hire car at an airport, a staff member stated that there would be a €100 charge for cleaning, owing to some of my dog's hairs being left in the car boot. The staff acknowledged that as there were few such hairs, he would like to be able to waive the charge, but did not have the authority to do so. Minutes later, on checking-in at the airport, I arrived with two large check-in items. The airline's staff member informed me that the booking was for just one, but she was prepared to check in both items and waive the extra €50 fee. My immediate respective feelings were such that I inclined not to use the car hire company in future, while the airline secured a loyal customer. Such seemingly small gestures and matters of policy demonstrate whether a culture places the customer at the centre.

The question of the degree to which customer-facing staff have the autonomy to override formal rules in a bid to provide an optimal service experience for the customer is a judgement that all executives must make. In this book, there is a conscious bias towards encouraging autonomy for staff and maintaining a service-based, rather than a rules-based, culture. If managers do not trust customer-facing staff to exercise good judgement in assisting customers and securing their loyalty without incurring excessive costs for the business, then the proper response is better recruitment and training of these key personnel, rather than tinkering endlessly with the rules.

Frustrating experiences for customers are quite common. Where a company prioritises setting rules and levying charges over helping the customer, it risks losing business. It may gain modest revenues in the short term, but only at the expense of brand reputation and customer retention. No matter how good your systems are, they might well fail to recover from the negative descriptions of a poor service to friends and family in conversations over the dinner table.

Viewing your processes from the customer's point of view becomes more important, and at times quite challenging, as technology advances. In theory, automated processes and online shopping make price comparisons when ordering goods or services more efficient for the provider, who can also offer a greater array of services more easily, more quickly and often more straightforwardly from the customer's point of view. Everyone can win, but only if the system is well designed – and by 'well designed', I mean from the customer's perspective, not in terms only of cost-saving for the provider or the ability to deploy the latest technology, or to up-sell a related product.

Previous chapters have emphasised the importance of cross-disciplinary collaboration, and nowhere is this more important than in ensuring a great experience for the customer. This perhaps especially includes areas where new technology opens new opportunities. The tech folk can tell you what the technology *can* do, but there should be a wider group decision as to what it *should* do. The starting point of discussions could be: 'What does the customer want and need? How can we enhance their experience?' The head of technology needs to be a member of the steering group, overseeing the introduction of the new technology, but they should not lead it. The process should be led and informed by a customer perspective.

There is an old saying in management education, though sadly not one that is always the guiding principle in designing customer service systems. It goes like this:

Customers in a DIY store don't really want a drill, they want a hole in the wall...

In fact, they don't really want a hole in the wall, they want somewhere to fit a screw...

Actually, they don't really want to fit a screw, they want to attach a bracket to the wall...

No, they don't really want a bracket on the wall, they want something to support a shelf...

Specifically, they don't really want a shelf, they want somewhere to put their books so that they don't take up room on the floor.

That is what the customer really wants – not a drill, but a convenient place for storing books. Understanding and relentlessly applying this concept is what it really means to understand a customer's needs. It requires empathy, arguably the most neglected attribute required by a top executive.

Businesses are established to provide solutions to customers' problems, and professionals who are specialists in design and delivery will have much expertise in – and enthusiasm for – what the latest products and services can deliver. However, this is often a very different perspective from that of the customer. For example, the IT and product design people may be keen to offer a sophisticated product with many options, while a customer may value simplicity. Service providers may be enthused about the cost efficiency of a chatbot, but for some needs a customer may wish to speak to a person instead. While generally, companies do offer a hybrid of both chatbots and access to a customer service member of staff, they may underestimate the collective work required to get the balance right and ensure that the customer can easily access the most appropriate channel. Likewise, ambitious sales targets may incentivise selling as many products as possible to new and existing customers, but if the sales tactics are not chosen with the customers' interests as the priority, they may become a nuisance and lead some customers to switch to another provider.

Prototyping, testing and responsible risk-taking
There is a way of working popularised in young tech firms in which rapid development, prototyping and live testing is used to accelerate innovation. The theory is that the appeal or viability of a product may be difficult to assess, so there may be more to learn from early roll-out, then responding to customer complaints in order to refine. While this method can be highly effective, it can be taken too far and brings the significant risk in a regulated sector that a non-compliant product may inadvertently be launched into the market. It is a more appropriate approach for, say, a video games company than one in financial services. It is not just a case of regulatory risk: there's a danger that the approach is pushed too strongly from the producer's view, rather than the user's perspective. Waiting for customer complaints is too passive, and there is significant risk of loss of trust and damage to the brand if problems are significant and remain uncorrected for an extended period. An alternative is to set up panels of customers and other forums that help to

educate internal managers, technologists, distribution staff and others on how the customers use the product, how they may wish to use it, and the features they may like to see offered in the future. This intelligence can be gathered prior to the launch and, of course, does not prevent further iterations thereafter.

A further initiative that the CEO can personally take is to experience at first hand a product that is in development. This might involve sitting at a computer to experience the development, sale and purchase of a prototype digital product, with the development team clustered around. This initiative can reveal several teething problems, and the learning will be simultaneous for all relevant team members.

It is best if development teams are kept small – around six people – so that there is real accountability and little opportunity to hide behind the hierarchy. You will want to motivate people to improve customer experience rather than make impressive presentations to a large internal group. The product development team should be multi-disciplinary and include someone who represents the customer's point of view (this is not the same as the distributor's point of view!).

A poorly designed product rushed into the marketplace can damage trust in the brand. In some sectors, the details of how the product is put together may be technically sophisticated. Customers do not have the time to work out how such a product is constructed; rather, they simply want assurances that it is safe and will reliably meet their needs. Trust in the brand can take years or even decades to build but can be lost relatively quickly. This point links directly to the discussion in Chapter 8 about consistency of principles and the importance of honesty and fair dealings. Just one breach of these can cause trust in the brand to falter or even collapse completely.

Also linked to this is the importance of upholding standards and values at all times. The CEO should be constantly prepared for the company to discipline any employee for breach of standards, including the high performers. This is key to upholding trust in the brand. Fundamental to the customer's expectation is wanting to be able to trust this company to be safe and responsible – especially where their products are complex, and where the impact of their failure would be severe, such as in transport, medical care or financial services.

Technology is an enabler – move quickly and don't skimp

The best technology is necessary but not sufficient for the best customer service, it is nevertheless important to remember that it *is* necessary. Inertia in an established way of working can set in remarkably quickly, and there is always a risk of complacency and failure to renew with smarter processes and better technology. In the context of enhancing customer service, a critical discipline is to be undeterred by the argument that 'the system won't let us'. It becomes an excuse. If it really is the case that there is a systemic barrier to better serving the customer, it's best to explore ways to remove it.

With access to adequate funding, an effective policy is for the CEO to announce that there will be no upper limit on investment in technology, provided the return justifies the investment. This only works if you have the right individual in post as Chief Technology Officer. A further safeguard is to ensure that technology upgrades and other technology projects are informed by the customer perspective.

This is effective as a policy because it means that where service improvements could be made with the right investment, they are put in place quickly and thoroughly, so the benefits are felt correspondingly quickly. If an investment can enhance the service and generate more returns, it is clearly better to implement those improvements as soon as possible, rather than successively postpone them. Don't limit your capacity artificially.

A related discipline is for the CEO to ask of the technology team (and other teams): 'What stops us from completing this project in half the time?' If the answer is 'Not enough staff', then see if you can find the budget to hire the extra staff. Generally, moving quickly and modernising quickly is the optimal way to continually improve service to the customer, as well as business performance more generally.

Moving quickly may appear to be a high-risk way of operating, but:

a. This is not the case if you have the right people in post and good teamwork, and;

b. Moving slowly usually comes with even greater risk.

Short lines of communication between customers and executives

Among the benefits of the open-plan office and the close team-working approach outlined in previous chapters is that there is more continuous, real-time updating of information and exchange of intelligence between managers and staff – and this includes customer-facing staff. Generally, it is valuable if senior executives are situated in close proximity to some customers. This can avoid the dislocation that may otherwise occur in the case of a large company with high levels of social distance between employees. Here, leaders could become overly reliant on written reports, which are poor substitutes for direct observations.

Once, as CEO in a retail company, I sat with the customer service staff for a period of a few months. As it was a walk-in customer centre, with customers attending in person, I was able to overhear the conversations. This provided a rich education on the complexity of many of the products and the reality of the customer's experience, which helped inform changes to simplify and improve this. Generally, in business management, product innovation is seen as a positive, but in this particular example there had been a proliferation of new products and changing product lines over the course of years.

All the products had their own rules, and the result was considerable complexity, which the customers often found difficult to deal with.

In addition to the direct learning for a CEO from such an initiative, this placement also sent out a signal to staff that the most senior executive in the company was committed to understanding and improving the customer experience, acting as a symbol of customer-centricity and showing associated direction.

Appoint a Chief Customer Officer and ensure they report to the CEO

It is unfortunately the case in many business sectors that employees who deal directly with customers do not have a high status. Arguably, this is illogical, especially if these organisations are serious about having a service-based ethos. Typically, finance, technology and marketing functions have the kudos.

One of the aims of the initiative of positioning myself next to customer service staff was to redress this perception. My direct learning of some of the issues facing customers, by listening to the conversations in real time, was not the only benefit: another was the signal it sent out to the wider organisation. At times, I've spent an entire Saturday listening to customers in a focus group and encouraged other leaders to engage directly with those using the company's services.

If an activity is prioritised, signalled and measured within a business, it is far more likely to be done, and done well. The appointment of a Chief Customer Officer (CCO) is another measure. Some companies claim to be customer-centric, yet while the heads of finance, technology and marketing report to the CEO, the CCO does not – or there isn't such a post.

The most effective CCOs typically have experience in more than one sector. They have learned to understand who the customer is, and what their needs are, in very different sectors, for different types of service, and in some cases experiencing both business-to-business and business-to-consumer operations. Experience in a highly volatile retail market, such as fashion, is valuable – that is, in sectors where companies do not survive if they fail to stay close to changing customer preferences.

Empathy and data are both necessary

Placing yourself closer to the customer – not necessarily physically close, but closer in terms of experience and understanding – provides an executive with information that neatly complements that which is available through analytics. There is a real risk, with the rapid advancements of AI models and other forms of automation, that executives rely exclusively on data for information. Data does not capture everything. It is necessary, but not sufficient. You don't know what you don't know. Data will tell you if a service has failed, but you need empathy to understand the impact on the customer: the ability to comprehend the difference between a ten-minute delay and cancellation of the last flight before a major public holiday; the depth of experience to understand that trust in the brand matters; and that serious breaches of trust imperil the very basis of the company's licence to operate.

Empathy and imagination are as important in business as technology and data. If all your executives have a scientific or finance background, perhaps hire someone who studied languages, drama, history or classics. A combination of all types of intelligence and learning offer the best opportunities especially with regards to understanding customers and markets. It is inadvisable to prize computational ability above emotional intelligence, although the reverse bias would also be unhelpful.

For understanding the customer experience, questionnaire replies can be helpful, but they often need to be treated with caution, and are best supplemented by deeper conversations. A regular customer may tone down their feelings of disappointment over poor service for fear that criticism may result in a further deterioration of standards. Customers are often incentivised to complete a question-naire by the reward of a small gift, which may further nudge them towards a flattering verdict. A net promoter score – which is an indi-cator of the relative proportion of customers who are enthusiastic about your products compared to detractors – is valuable informa-tion. It is best seen as a starting point for deeper investigations.

Direct conversations, in-depth and focused on the real customer experience, provide an essential complement to data. There is a risk when listening to a small group that they may be unrepresentative, but this risk can be mitigated. For example, the CEO can encourage all senior managers, and other key employees, to engage in such conversations, in order to create engagement collectively with a larger group. Also, a specialist Head of Customer Service will have knowledge and expertise in putting together representative focus groups.

Rotation of posts, described in earlier chapters, is relevant here. It is helpful for all senior executives to have at least some experience in a customer-facing role. For example, when a highly customer-centric marketing specialist was appointed head of Customer Service and proceeded to reorientate the whole operational base of the company based on the customer's point of view, they found that some of the most important sources of frustration for customers were to do with delays and lack of responsiveness. This resulted in measures to reduce the number of hand-offs and to get routine requests and complaints sorted quickly. The company started measuring turn-around times in minutes rather than days. This had a dramatic and accelerating effect. It was discovered that a major bottleneck was the mailroom, at a time when there was still important communication via conventional post despite significant email and web-based communication. A specialist leader was hired from a global parcel delivery specialist and within weeks he had improved efficiency by 90%.

What the customer really wants may disappoint you

From a product provider's point of view, you will rightly be innovating, learning about new technology and the latest techniques in management theory, and understanding how they may be deployed in your company. This does not mean, however, that the newest technology or most sophisticated approach is always optimal for your customers.

Decades ago, we were attempting to enhance customers' options by offering them the opportunity to top-up their original product. It ended up being administratively complicated to set this up, and not always easy for the customer to navigate. The more effective alternative proved to be simply offering the customer an additional product. From our product provider's perspective, it felt like an inelegant solution, compared with the intellectually rewarding challenge of creating a single adjustable flexible product. However, the adopted approach addressed the customer's needs, with both less complexity and a corresponding lower cost for all parties than the more elegant alternative.

This leads on to an important consideration, that of customer segmentation. This is, of course, an area with considerable literature from the discipline of marketing, but it is worth a brief discussion here.

Customer segmentation

A combination of capturing data on customer experience and preferences, information from focus groups and other interactions, and the appointment of a specialist Chief Customer Officer combine to provide a valuable body of intelligence. An established discipline that helps make sense of this knowledge and inform strategies and tactics is customer segmentation – dividing the actual and potential customer population into identifiable constituencies whether grouped by age, income level, or other factors such as risk appetite or other aspects of personal taste.

It helps to define identifiable segments within the markets you are seeking to serve. It is as important to identify those you are *not* aiming to serve as those that you are. If your services are not suitable for elderly people, then you should make sure you're not marketing to that demographic. Trying to appeal to all members of society equally is not realistic or viable in most circumstances. For instance, in the case of financial services you may identify that a segment of customers is made up of people aged 45-55 on a middle income, not close to retirement age but aware of a need to boost pension savings, with a medium-ranked preference on risk appetite. Try to build up a picture of a customer in the mid-point of the distribution curve of a targeted customer segment and ask: What are their desires, preferences, values and fears? How are they likely to access your products and services, and what can be done to improve their experiences? How are their needs likely to change in the future?

Summary

In the 2020s, with many technologists and venture capitalists investing in virtual or mixed reality headsets and space travel, much of the economic world is experiencing rising costs-of-living, high healthcare costs and long hospital waiting lists, a lack of housing, and job insecurity. Dealing with what customers actually want or need can at times be disappointing for the ambitious CEO. You may discover that they don't want the latest technology, they just want something affordable, accessible and reliable. Customers want things not to break down – and they don't like unexpected surcharges.

This is not to discourage technological innovation, because inventions can help you meet customers' needs, often dramatically enhancing their experience. However, you have little chance of meeting their needs and preferences if you do not know what these are.

Working back from the customer's needs is, like all worthwhile executive strengths, an approach that requires considerable thought and discipline. It is not achieved solely by looking at net promotor scores and other information on marketing dashboards, although accurate and up-to-date data on customer preference and behaviour is essential. A strong comprehension of the business's ultimate reason to exist, for example to enhance quality of life for the customer, should underlie your approach. Close team-working and the shortest possible lines of communication between customers and senior executives, and upholding values of honest dealing, are essential practices.

CHAPTER 13
CULTURE IS THE BUSINESS

Chapters 8 and 9 covered the elements of a high-engagement, high-performance business culture, including a discussion of the puzzle as to why it still isn't the norm, nor the automatic aspiration of all business leaders. One of the reasons is the persistence of approaches to business management that regard short-term targets and financial results as the main points of focus, which disregards people and in which relationships are deemed to be a 'softer' consideration, rather than being regarded as the ultimate source of all value. This results in the catchphrase of some highly effective humanitarian business leaders: *'Do the right thing; just don't get caught!'*

This perspective points to some deeper questions around tacit beliefs and operating assumptions that are worthy of intellectual challenge – a theme that was explored in interviews I carried out with former senior executive colleagues in preparation for this book. There is a shared belief among the participants in these conversations - an understanding that organisational culture *is* the business. It isn't a separate category owned by the HR department or to be attended to only on a few occasions during the year when you're thinking about teams on a managerial away day.

An approach our interviewees take issue with, is one of segregation – assuming that people and culture belong in one category, while strategy and business results belong in another. It is more effective to treat the issues in a thoroughly integrated way.

A very high priority for the CEO is to ensure the highest levels of functional excellence in all department leaders. It is also important that these individuals combine this functional expertise with a broader commercial awareness and ability to work in teams, understanding the perspectives of other specialisms. It pays to hire a CFO who understands the importance of culture, and a Head of HR who can read a balance sheet and understands the business's money-making logic.

Sheela Parakkal, a former colleague of mine and Chief HR Officer (CHRO), likes to seize opportunities to put some of her principles into practice. The emphasis on employing the right people, linked to a strong sense of purpose, had a direct effect on performance. She adds:

"If an organisation is focused on what really matters – that is, who we are and how we show up as an organisation, as a collective, you actually get the results. I mean, prior to this experience I had read about the whole connection about culture and performance, but I can safely say [now] that I've experienced it in my lifetime and my career."

This means relishing the challenges, as well as the opportunities, that such an approach entails. If the initiatives of the HR function are integrated fully into operations and performance management, this results in a high degree of responsibility and accountability, with consequences if policies do not prove to be effective. There needs to be a business purpose, rather than training or activities around 'culture' that are not linked to commercial results. The move towards team-working and the open plan office was part of a regeneration of performance, not a social experiment.

From the Chief Finance Officer's perspective, Andreas Rosenthal, who has worked as CFO with me in more than one business, agrees. He challenges the assumption that 'culture' is a discrete activity owned by HR. Rather, it should be seen as a synonym for the business generally. "Culture is not a project," he says, adding:

"Culture is not something where you say, for example, that from January to August you do culture – followed by a switch where you say, 'Now, let's get back to business.' Many organisations do that. What you actually need to say is that culture *is* the business. It is not a project, it is part of every day, which means you need to speak to the culture at every interaction."

In practice, this means challenging people when they fail to live up to the standards required to maintain a healthy culture. If the expectation is that the business exhibits a supportive, team-based, collaborative culture, then a manager who displays rude behaviour or shields information from another department unreasonably needs to be challenged. When a healthy culture is well established, the organisation can collectively curb such uncooperative behaviours, even when they are exhibited by a senior individual. Andreas observes:

"So initially, you would probably see that the C-suite executive from the top will intervene, but over time, when the culture is strong, it will self-regulate."

Andreas describes how a new, co-created and well-established culture can then be maintained over time:

"In terms of how we operate from a values perspective, from the culture, how we engage is exactly the same. There is no change to the way people collaborate, to the way in which people think about collective responsibility. People empower, people engage, people challenge and so forth. And, it doesn't even mean that it's the same people – we have a lot of new people now. The culture is so embedded that when someone new is considering joining, if at the point of interview they indicate that they want a more traditional culture – for example a separate office – then they just don't join.

When you create the culture in a shared way, and make it sustainable, it is not dependent on a leader. It's something that becomes almost in the DNA of the firm."

Data is the compass, not the journey

Organisations cannot be purely 'data-led'. Humans are a narrative species: we make sense of the world through stories. We need facts, but they are always instinctively, inherently woven into a narrative. Accurate and relevant data must be a central guide to assessing business performance, but data is the compass, not the journey.

In addition, humans are social and emotional beings; we need to bond to other humans – which is why solitary confinement is a punishment. A central understanding in group and individual psychology is the concept of attachment. This informs the principle of 'move slow to move fast', described in earlier chapters. To build teams and social cohesion, be aware that too much change creates too much loss, resulting in a potentially dangerous loss of psychological safety, in turn damaging cohesion and direction. Teams require conscious acts of social building, the core practices of which are described in earlier chapters; they do not occur simply by saying, 'You are a team'.

An optimal approach to leadership is based on an understanding of the role of both data and narratives as essential and complementary. As a leader, you are well advised to lean into human reality. People are often described as the 'most important asset' in a business, but this is an understatement and a mis-categorisation. People do not comprise an asset class – rather, they are the living agents who will or will not ensure that you achieve your business aims. Andreas Rosenthal observes:

> "I hate it when sometimes people say our people are our greatest asset. It makes it sound as though people are a stock or a bond which you can buy and sell anytime... When someone says, 'What is the culture?', it's the people. A good culture means that when you speak to ten people in the company, you get a sense of this common fabric, which binds us together in how we operate."

When major technical or other errors occur in a way that affects customers, this will naturally result in considerable upset and even protest. The story might even reach the news. As CEO, it is essential to issue a full and unqualified apology – if necessary, aired on national media. Whatever the cause of the issue, taking care of affected customers should be the priority, and should be seen as such to protect both the reputation of the company and the brand.

I recall a technical fix involving many hours of laborious work in the technology department. It needed to be overseen by the Chief Technology Officer, but though the work was relatively routine, it was more detailed than appropriate for his expertise. He therefore didn't have much to do. As people were working late into the evening, he decided to take orders from everyone for their preferred pizza. The experience of a C-suite executive ordering and fetching dozens of pizzas for his team was a vivid illustration of the concept of 'servant leadership'. In terms of short-term operational efficiency, it didn't add much value; in terms of longer-term building of a powerful culture, it was priceless. Years later, what people remember is the pizza being served by the CTO, more than the technical fixes that were necessary. That story is in the business. Businesses need data, but they need folklore too.

A sense of purpose and direction

Another core human trait is our need to have a strong sense of 'why' as well as 'what' in our everyday working lives. That is, we need a sense of purpose to unite the two drives discussed earlier in this chapter: our story-telling nature and our need to bond. The stories that guide us need to make sense of the enterprise in which we are individually and collectively engaged, so that we feel we are making a positive difference.

Understanding where the customer is coming from, what their needs are and how the organisation can fulfil them, is not only helpful for continual enhancement of service, but also inculcates a sense of collective purpose within the organisation. A healthy sense of purpose is couched in terms of enhancing financial security for citizens, or enabling people to be fitter and healthier, or giving people opportunities to travel and meet people, or protecting an ecosystem. It is less helpful, and probably disempowering, to explain the purpose in terms of meeting financial targets.

A CEO needs to have a strong sense of the fundamental question: 'Why do we exist as an organisation?', and in turn help spread the understanding of this purpose throughout the employee population. It can be helpful to facilitate discussions on this. This does not mean delegating strategy-setting to the wider employee population, it means chairing internal discussions that enable a wider under-standing of the business's core purpose, its social contract, or reason for existing. CEOs cannot give a running commentary on all the busi-ness's activities, but they should communicate clearly and consistently enough regarding the overall strategy and objectives. Individuals and teams should not experience significant surprises regarding announcements relating to core objectives or values. These should be well understood – as in Andreas' description of being able to ask ten individuals from different parts of the business about the values and ways of working and receive broadly similar answers from each.

Sheela Parakkal describes the importance of 'getting down to why we exist as an organisation'. This means collectively addressing fundamental questions, such as:

"Who do we serve? How do we show up? How does that translate into how we operate? How does that translate to the people, the leaders we need? And taking actions consistent with that, for me, and for the organisation, was so important for us [at the time] to turn the corner on business performance. Because you don't do all of this just for the sake of personal purpose and alignment or looking good from a theory perspective. You do this because you get results."

The 'North Star' is fairness

Also emerging from discussions with former colleagues were some insightful ideas around the links between a leader's conduct and the organisation's sense of purpose – where the individual and the collective interact. The cognitive and emotional challenge for the leader described in *Chapter 6: Mental Agility*, involving the ability to switch between empathy and decisiveness, is less of a challenge if the binding concepts are fairness and the long-term business interest. If a unit must be closed to ensure viability of the business, this decision will save more jobs than it costs.

Another example of making tough decisions in the interests of the business is dismissing people who do not live up to the culture and values. Andreas Rosenthal observes:

> "I don't see it as a contradiction to say you're nurturing, you're empathetic while also being able to make tough decisions. I've always said this to people when they say, 'Andreas, isn't it tough that you let these and these people go?' And my answer is always: Can you imagine how unfair it would be to the 100 other people following the culture to keep someone who isn't?"

He goes on to observe that most organisations are more unforgiving of poor business performance than poor cultural fit, but questions this priority. If anything, it pays to uphold the culture more strongly, because it is ultimately a powerful collective source of added value. Individual performance can be worked on, but once the culture begins to fray, it can deteriorate in an uncontrolled way.

Arjun Mallik, a CEO and former colleague, makes a similar point, saying that the 'North Star' governing a leader's decisions is fairness, and this determines whether to be sympathetic or tough:

> "If you're able to hold opposing views in your mind, if you're able to deploy experience, creativity and communication skills effectively, then you *will* find a solution. And when adjudicating on trade-offs, disputes and competing opinions, fairness is the 'go-to' leadership quality to rely on. Principles-based, consistent, and fair decision making creates maturity in a team (other leaders emulate this behaviour), and creates an environment where choices and feedback are about the quality of the work, and rarely a criticism of individuals – a hallmark of personality-based political corporate cultures."

Summary

Culture isn't something 'out there'. It isn't a project, an HR initiative or something reserved for an offsite team-building exercise. It is what you, and everyone in the business, do and say daily. A healthy culture, based on operational effectiveness and focused on the overriding purpose of enhancing the customer's quality of life, upheld continuously, is the single most valuable source of operational strength.

CHAPTER 14
COMMUNICATION IS THE LIFEBLOOD

A CEO who says that 'the customer comes first' will typically have a Chief Customer Officer. A CEO who says that employees are the most important asset and that engaging them is a priority, will generally have the head of HR reporting directly to them. A CEO asserting the importance of communication will typically have a senior-level head of communication. These tendencies reflect a conscious bias discussed earlier in the book, in which people and culture are attended to in a central or strategic way.

Communication is a core responsibility of the CEO. Probably, most executives understand the importance of communicating the main narrative, linked to strategic objectives, and that the responsibilities around communication extend much further than that. All the CEO's statements – formal and informal, in both public speeches and asides made in the corridor – have influence. This does not mean you should be carefully polishing every word, risking over-analysis of all statements and a consequent paralysis, but it does help to avoid being flippant or over-communicating. Your words will be analysed and will become the subject of comment and gossip, so it is best to keep things clear and straightforward. Communication is not just about formal statements to a wider audience, but also about how you address meetings, how you talk to direct reports (for example, when you are setting their objectives and evaluating their performance), and how you conduct yourself more generally.

Everyone in the business needs to know what the purpose and strategic aims are, with clear personal performance targets linked to these. This requires consistent and strong communicative ability by the CEO, functional heads, and the professional communications team. Business writer John Kotter has set out an eight-step process for leading change, and has observed that most leaders need to increase their communication by a factor of around ten. This does not imply long speeches and communiques: short, frequent and consistent messaging is the most effective.

Clarity and brevity

It helps to try to convey the same message in similar ways to different audiences. Employees and others will pick up on inconsistencies. You need to be prepared to bore yourself somewhat by consistently repeating the same essential messages about strategy and objectives. Even seemingly minor alterations in messaging or emphasis can be unsettling and lead to misinterpretation by the teams. The messages should be as brief and as clear as possible, while still articulating the way forward.

In line with the principle of brevity, a helpful discipline is to avoid over-announcing. In other words, only publish a press release or make a formal internal announcement if there is something of substance to say. It is fine not to make such statements every week. The very act of committing to a formal statement, internal or external, is significant in itself. If the message has little real substance – if it's mostly platitudes, for example: well-meaning but vague declarations of general principles – it will fall a little flat. The audience may begin speculating about what the 'real' message is meant to be, assuming there must some intended meaning that requires interpretation. Alternatively, if they begin to ignore official statements, this could become a habit and you will have lost a section of your audience when you do need to communicate something important.

Sentences should be short, with clarity around who the key personnel are and where responsibilities lie. To this end, it is better to avoid the passive voice as a linguistic device, especially where something has gone wrong. If for example you say 'mistakes were made', this is evasive and comes across as a desire to escape accountability. It is better always to be specific, without unfairly naming individuals or placing blame. The CEO should apologise personally and directly if there has been a service failure, especially one that directly affects the public – irrespective of whether the CEO themself was personally involved in making mistakes at an operational level. This is part of your job description; if it occurred on your watch, you take responsibility.

Internally, within meetings, presentations should be short, practical and to the point. A wasteful habit to avoid is that of long presentations: the tendency to demonstrate knowledge rather than propose actions. Meetings should be short, strongly chaired, and focused (see *Chapter 9*, **Principles for Effective Meetings**). If the actions are clear and there is little discussion required, be prepared to close a meeting after five or ten minutes, so that people can get back to value-adding activities.

The CEO will frequently give formal talks to the board, to journalists, at a conference, and so on. It is a worthwhile investment to devote some time to crafting a talk. This does not mean the talk should be long – much of the preparation time may be spent removing superfluous words and ensuring the language is clear and concise. It helps to focus on the essential priorities, asking questions such as:

- What do I really want to say?
- Do I really need to say it to this audience?
- How can I sound positive yet also realistic?
- What level of detail do they need – what might be better communicated in writing?
- What are the likely effects of my words on the audience?
- How does the messaging fit with the overall strategy and help us meet our goals?

Speak and write clearly

I am a native English speaker and have spent most of my career, including many of my CEO roles, in countries that are non-English-speaking. Straightforwardness and clarity of language are essential disciplines in general, but even more so when most of the audience is reading or listening in their second or third language. It is always helpful to keep emails short and to the point. In one instance, I discovered that an employee had been asking a family member to help translate emails from English into their own language. If important emails from the CEO or other executives are long, containing non-essential information, this causes avoidable stress. The CEO is a role model: if their written messages are short and to the point, then this is likely to become a habit throughout the organisation.

Another essential discipline for the native speaker is to curb the tendency – quite pronounced in the managerial class in the English-speaking world – to use metaphorical phrases such as 'blue-sky thinking', 'boiling the ocean', 'moving the needle', and so on. By definition, a metaphor is not a description of reality, but a description of what reality can be compared to. On occasion, it may provide a vivid image that helps underline an important point – indeed, the title of this chapter is a metaphor, consciously chosen to emphasise the importance of communication by asserting that the company can cease to exist if communication fails. However, a metaphor should not serve as a replacement for an accurate description of business reality, nor of essential definitions and job descriptions. It is better to describe the actual responsibilities of individuals, and the type of meetings and their frequency, and identify the key personnel you plan to deploy, than to use metaphorical terms such as 'framework' or 'structure'.

Along with metaphor, there are other verbal habits in the English-speaking world, particularly the UK, that can obstruct clear communication. Prominent among these are sarcasm and understatement. Below are some examples of these three types of unclear and often unhelpful communication in response to a development in the workplace.

Metaphor – The executives have identified a need to anticipate changes in the market: '*We need to skate where the puck is heading.*'

Understatement – The company wins a prestigious award, or becomes a market leader: '*Well, we've had worse days.*'

Sarcasm – There has been a succession of customer complaints following a service failure: '*I'm going to put you lot forward for Customer Service of the Year award.*'

Such comments may appear wryly amusing, in the case of sarcasm and understatement, but they prevent full and proportionate communication to the team from the executive. They can cause misunderstanding and stress in a community where the cultural norms are different, and your language is the second language of the receiver.

A senior manager is not a poet or stand-up comedian. Communication is a means to an end. For most essential communication, it is better to be boring and clear than funny and ambiguous. Employee engagement tends to be derived more from teamwork and accomplishment, fulfilling the customer's needs, than from entertaining speeches by the CEO. However, as with most aspects of leadership, it is good to strike a balance. It does not help to be robotic in delivery and a joke can lighten the mood. As with metaphor, so with humour – a touch of it here and there can be effective, but it should not be used to *replace* important communications about strategy, performance and objectives.

Positive framing

Choice of terminology has a direct and often significant impact on culture and performance. Employees are likely to be confused and uninspired if you are falsely positive, using vague terminology. But it helps to stay calm in a crisis and see the positive options in all circumstances.

Here is a simple example of how seemingly minor changes to vocabulary can help lift the team in the face of bad news. If a business decides to curb some wasteful ways of working, or to end an initiative, or close a unit, it is common to use phrases such as 'cost-cutting' or even 'slashing', which are negative and direct the listener to what is being lost, rather than to what is being gained. They may even generate fear that the business is retrenching and in a process of decline. It is often possible to substitute with terms such as 'efficiency' and 'effectiveness', which convey focus and help maintain a sense that improvement and progress are taking place, rather than cutbacks and loss.

Even in a crisis, you can often identify something positive by addressing the reality of the situation and its impact on people, including employees or customers.

Explaining the 'why'

Closely linked to the theme of positive framing is the responsibility of the CEO to explain the rationale for certain objectives, or strategies, or changes of policy. It may be seen as a superfluous activity by some, who may feel that only the C-suite need to understand the ultimate purpose, but this is a mistake. In some cases, where the products are sophisticated and the markets unpredictable, an explanation may be lengthy.

The reason for this is that human beings are a sense-making species. If deprived of an explanation for the purpose of an activity, we will instinctively speculate. Given a choice between understanding the real reason and an invented one, it is always better for staff to know the real purpose. Ping Ping Tan, a Corporate Communications Head and former colleague of mine, says:

> "Every piece of communication did not just contain the *what*, the news. We were always very keen to highlight *why* we were doing certain things. The *why* was important in the case for change. That was central to all communication."

The link to employee engagement in understanding the purpose is researched and understood. People are more likely to be enthusiastic and committed if they feel that there is some social purpose, some way in which they are enhancing quality of life for customers, rather than being told: 'Just do this and you'll get paid', with the proviso that this sense of purpose should not replace good employment conditions and will often not be the central motivator in an employee's life (see Chapter 9, sub-heading *Can an organisation become too engaged?*).

Understanding the wider impact of your services and activities can help in other ways too. In-depth discussions of purpose can help improve service design and delivery, as well as regulatory compliance and company reputation. Developing and articulating the *why*, assisted by frequent internal discussions, to encompass better use of finite resources, is crucial in informing decision making. It reduces the risks of making policy errors, of harming customers, and of incurring penalties for regulatory breaches.

The only occasion when it may be sensible to downplay the 'real' reason for a decision is when managing someone out of the organisation who has not been guilty of misconduct, perhaps where there is a skills mismatch or a consistent failure to meet objectives. Here, it is invariably possible to let the individual decide the narrative around their departure and allow them to leave with their reputation intact.

Communication is a profession

I have been questioned over the priority I give to communication, and the level of investment entailed in establishing and running well-resourced communications departments. A Chief Finance Officer on one occasion has observed to me: "Why do your communications teams typically cost more than in other companies?" The answer is that the outlay is conceived as an investment, rather than a net cost. As with other features of the high-engagement culture, these sceptical questions tend to subside once the positive commercial results come in and are maintained.

The recommendation of this book is that the Head of Communications should report directly to the CEO. This is by no means universal practice. Sometimes, the communications function is part of the marketing department, which reflects an underestimation of its importance. Communication is not just about marketing and relating the strategy – it is about everything.

I have found that marketing professionals are sometimes not the best communicators, and it is generally preferable to recruit as communications professionals people who have a journalistic or other more directly communication-focused background. They are skilled in language and are quickly able to identify the essential story that needs communicating – 'What's the headline?' – and often bring with them a useful wider network. The same communications team should be responsible for both internal and external communications. It is a sign of organisational integrity that the respective messages are broadly the same. There will typically be less that you can divulge publicly, but it is a warning sign of organisational dysfunction if press statements diverge significantly from internal reality. Since the advent of social media, it's likely that information will leak out in any event. And if there's a message that you wish to disseminate publicly but your press release attracts little interest, then an old trick that often works is to include the information in an internal message labelled 'highly confidential'.

In a similar way, it is a healthy sign if the messaging to the regulator is consistent with press releases and internal messages; a specialist comms team can often help draft communication for a regulatory body. An internal function is often more effective than using a PR agency, for similar reasons – the individuals are part of the organisational culture and values.

With a well-resourced, specialist corporate communications team, is there a risk that the communications responsibilities and abilities of heads of departments and other important managers are neglected, with everything left to the communications team? This would appear to be a possibility, but it is very much the case of it being 'both/and', not 'either/or'. It does not undermine the authority of the heads of functions if the CEO, or the comms team, bypass the line managers and communicate directly to the wider employee population – provided that the messages are consistent and helpful, without contradicting or undermining a manager.

Relying solely on functional heads to communicate could limit cross-departmental conversations (see also *Chapter 10: Open Plan Offices*). It is better to encourage a wider range of conversations to support collaboration. Moreover, because some heads of functions are likely to be better than others at communication, devolving most of the responsibility of communication to them would result in some departments being much better informed than others.

Good practice tips: One tactic that works effectively is to encourage functional heads to invite other functional heads to their own town hall meetings. In this way, it isn't only the finance function who understand the company finances; it isn't only the marketing people who know who we're marketing to and how – and so on.

Another tactic that can be effective is to add an element of fun to the town hall meetings, so that people want to attend, rather than feel obliged. Meetings don't have to feature long speeches by senior executives or presentations, they don't even have to be held in the office. You can offer refreshments and entertainment, include a celebration, and offer different ways of communicating narratives about the business, and generating ideas about its future. Ping Ping Tan recollects:

> "We experimented with different ways of communications and created unique, memorable experiences to tell the transformation story.
>
> For example, we created an art gallery to launch and communicate our purpose and values. We had employees of all levels and from different divisions on stage to present, so it wasn't just the CEO or the leaders who were sharing. These employees were early adopters of the purpose and change agents, so their stories were passionate and – importantly – more authentic."

Curbing gossip and factions

It is healthy to minimise secrets and rumours within an organisation. On occasion, you may hear your direct report begin to complain about the conduct of a colleague. At that point, you could intervene to caution them that any negative comment will be communicated to the person in question. Likewise, indicate that if you complain about a peer in an email, that colleague will be copied in the response. This comes as a shock to some people who expect lines of communication to run vertically only – up and down, between the manager and the CEO. Switching to a culture of transparency encourages those who are disagreeing to sort out their problems, and thus causes rumours and faction-forming to be minimised.

It is a compulsory requirement of the CEO to be an effective communicator It is not a 'nice-to-have' extra. If a manager is not communicating effectively, this may be either because they lack the ability, or because they are withholding themselves, cognitively and emotionally – they're not committed to the strategy. Either way, a sustained and significant failure to communicate must be addressed and in some cases the individual might have to be managed out of the organisation. For those with commitment but who lack ability, it is possible to arrange coaching to improve communication abilities. Again, this is best seen as an investment, not a cost.

Non-verbal communication

The way you conduct yourself as a senior executive conveys information to the employee population. The example of the CEO positioning himself next to the customer service team, reported in *Chapter 10: The Open Plan Office*, sent a strong message that they were committed to understanding the business and the level of service – that customer service was a priority. The decision to operate with an open plan layout informed the people in the business that cross-departmental communication was a priority whilst empty symbols of status were not.

There are other, smaller ways that the CEO can communicate through decisions. In *Chapter 7: Responsible Authority*, we discussed how the CEO's decisions about whom to talk to, and whom to socialise with, can convey messages – which may be misunderstood – regarding favoured cliques. It is advisable to avoid close relationships with a favoured few, which can be corrosive. A CEO needs to have a democratic spirit, and be fair-minded. The personal support network should not involve direct reports.

Body language will also be observed and interpreted. A CEO with hunched shoulders and a tendency to hide in an office will likely confuse and/or demoralise employees. You need to be available – but of course, not *too* available.

Your actions and words must support each other. There's little point in saying something is important, if you do not treat it as important – for example, if you make an official announcement about the importance of communication and transparency but then hide in a private office for a few weeks.

Communication in a hybrid working environment

The open plan office offers a physical environment that encourages cross-departmental communication and a high degree of collaboration. When you are not physically in the same building, how do you maintain this?

It helps to return to the point made at the beginning of *Chapter 1*. You should conceive of the organisation as a network of relationships held together by communication, not a structure with assets. This is both more accurate and more humane.

Summary

The ability to communicate effectively is not the ability to add flourishing touches to the executive's verbal repertoire – rather, it is a core discipline and skill. The whole enterprise needs to know and understand what their purpose is and what their objectives are, and be empowered to deliver them. When these are well understood across the business, executive decisions are likely to make sense and be accepted, on decisions such as which customer segments to target, and so on. There will be few surprises and individuals are more likely to be committed and engaged. Moreover, communication between and within specialisms must be maintained at a healthy level. Frequent, brief and consistent communication is the most effective style.

It is of course possible to communicate too much, leaving insufficient time for delivery, and so it is a quality to be optimised, in keeping with other disciplines and the theme of this book. Under-communicating is a more common problem in managers, however, especially those with a high level of technical expertise, than over-communicating. If in doubt, tell it again.

AFTERWORD
OBSERVATIONS ON OPTIMAL HUMILITY

"Your strength is also your weakness" – Anon.

This book has sought both to describe the realities of organisational leadership in a large international business in the early 21St Century, and to show how long-established concepts around the importance of teamwork and empowerment can be made to work.

There is a practical focus here, but given the nuances and complexities that are involved, I have not intended to write an instruction guide for the 'right' way for a CEO to run an enterprise. The benefits of certain timeless principles are clear and evidence-based – for example, being decisive about strategic direction, being honest with your staff, appointing people with the best expertise in particular roles, and involving all staff as team members. However, the style of honouring these principles will depend upon the organisational context and the personality of the leader.

While this book is far from being the first to emphasise the value of such practices, I was prompted to write it after observing that such practices are still far from commonplace. *Chapters 8* and *9* discuss some of the reasons for this. Indeed, at times it seems as though there are two different business worlds: the one of business schools, conference talks and literature, where the discussion is about engaging leadership, building collaborative teams and emotional intelligence; and a mostly contradictory real business world.

It is more than a quarter of a century since Professor Jeffrey Pfeffer was able to report a substantial evidence base supporting the principles emphasised in this book – managing through the team, ensuring psychological safety, honesty in dealings and communication. If we wish to be honest with ourselves in the managerial profession, it is worth asking the question, 'Why has there been so little progress?' As argued in this book, it is possible to overestimate the impact of a restructure and underestimate the impact of a change of personnel, indicating an underlying belief that the company is a structure, whereas in fact it consists of people. A company's structure is often no more than a mental construct or a metaphor, without a tangible presence in the real world.

These are also issues of leadership development that business schools might wish to address. As leaders, we could step outside of the bubble and be more self-reflective. Yes, we may feel we inspire our teams, but do we regard team building as central, rather than peripheral? Do we still secretly believe that engaging employees is 'the soft stuff', or that 'culture' is something for the corporate away day or the HR department?

Arguably, many business leaders are stronger in the crucially important areas of identifying market opportunities and under-standing the commercial logic of a business than on practising team-building and empowerment. Much of the literature that does emphasise the importance of such human dimensions has been written by academics. Their research findings help us understand the dynamics involved, and have been hugely informative for many, including myself. I hope that complementing these with a book by a practising executive might encourage further focus and priority on the implementation of high-engagement, high-performance practices, as well as including practical advice on specific approaches that I have been found to be effective.

Leadership is a human task, involving human emotions. We may deploy artificial intelligence and robots, but ultimately, we're still people seeking to serve other people. Sometimes – perhaps often – acting in a leadership role doesn't *feel* like leadership. It can feel rather messy and uncontrolled. As a CEO, effectively dealing with people is the route to organisational success, because ultimately people *are* your most valuable asset – all other assets are devalued without human agency. Nevertheless, people can of course be difficult to deal with. To return to an analogy used previously, as a leader you are like the conductor of an orchestra, in that you must direct and nurture a harmonious performance from a team of specialists. However, the real world and real markets are less controlled than a concert hall, and corporate salespeople and marketing specialists are typically not as disciplined as violinists.

I would like to finish by addressing some personal challenges I have encountered in attempting to practise the leadership approach I have advocated here.

I've emphasised the importance of finding an optimal balance on a range of matters: optimal autonomy; optimal pace of change; optimal balance between individual decision-making and devolving to the team. I have found this to be a constant challenge, testing my abilities and personal capacity. Achieving the optimal balance requires constant attention. Much of the time, I've felt I may have been getting it at least slightly wrong, then compensating, or slightly over-compensating. You may achieve the optimal balance over time, in aggregate, but it's never easy.

I have often been a Western CEO in an East Asian country, sometimes with a multi-national team reporting to me. Handling cultural differences has been a daily issue for me for more than two decades. While cultural differences can be hugely significant, I've also discovered that there is real commonality across cultures. For example, some observers understandably feared that my decision to make a switch to team-based working, with low hierarchy and an open plan office, would not work in East Asian countries where the cultures are often more formal and hierarchical than further West. What I learned is that effective teamwork as a route to success is a universal concept, in business as well as in sport.

While belief systems do differ in important elements, there is a widespread understanding of the value of empathy, to 'do as you would be done by', and on the nature of paradox, including the way in which humility, counter-intuitively, can help you become an effective leader. This has been one of the most sensitive challenges for me on which to optimise: the balance between displaying confidence and humility. My upbringing and faith have led me to cherish humility, but with experience I have learned that it is a disservice to the community to be too humble, as it can prevents offering your skills and abilities to the benefit of others.

At times, I have wondered if you could flick a switch between authoritativeness and humility, or even find a dimmer switch. In this book, I have sought to achieve a balance between these opposing ideas by using the phrase *responsible authority* (see *Chapter 7*). You must be clear about the areas that are in your zone of expertise, and properly within your realm of responsibility, and those which are not. You must have a clear understanding of your strengths, and the limits of your strengths – to know when to say, 'I can take the lead on this', and when to defer to someone else or engage in further consultation.

Another dimension is the acknowledgement that, as leaders, we sometimes get things wrong. We can become confident, and then overconfident. This book encourages you to be innovative, launching initiatives. Rather than every initiative succeeding, I prefer to have more initiatives in play, with only three fifths flourishing. Nevertheless, on occasion this can lead to individuals and teams becoming overburdened.

To a certain extent, this is inevitable in a volatile world. If you feel that you're in control, and that everything is running smoothly, you're probably missing something. Technology is constantly changing. Social media and automated intelligence tools can rapidly change markets, and routes to market, and opportunities for efficiency. In this book, I seek to encourage leaders to be continually innovative, and prepared to think afresh, never to feel satisfied. It is worth recognising the reality that if you have the healthy discipline of not being satisfied, you're naturally always going to feel at least a little dissatisfied. So, being an effective organisational leader is neither a fully satisfying nor an entirely comfortable place.

It can also be physically tiring. For example, as CEO of a region spanning two continents, it was often the case that, when I woke up, I didn't know which country I was in. In one phase, I would even fall asleep at night, not expecting to know where I was on waking up.

While an executive role is demanding, the CEO is in a fortunate position and is not a victim. Nevertheless, it is in your interests – and in the interests of the business and your family – that you don't collapse. There's a reason your car has a service, a rest and repair every few thousand miles. You need to do the same for yourself.

These are my findings: be bold; be innovative; make big calls; appoint the right people; delegate well; and empower your team.

And stay humble.

ABOUT THE AUTHOR

Wilf Blackburn is a 'serial' business leader, having held seven diverse Regional and Country CEO roles in the life and health insurance sector throughout Asia and Africa during the first quarter of the 21st Century. During this time, Wilf lived and worked in Hong Kong, Malaysia, the Philippines, PR China, Singapore, Thailand and Vietnam, whilst also serving on company Boards in Cambodia, Ghana, India, Indonesia, Kenya, Nigeria and Taiwan.

Wilf's work has primarily involved delivering large-scale and high-impact organisation-wide transformations alongside significant and sustained business growth.

A mathematician by training, Wilf began his professional career in the mid-1980s in London, initially as an actuary, prior to working in several other functions, including Finance, M&A, Strategy, Marketing, Distribution, and Programme Management, before becoming a generalist.

Wilf has been a perennial business school student, having been awarded post-graduate qualifications from INSEAD, Bath University, Oxford University and City University, London.

ACKNOWLEDGEMENTS

While living in Southeast Asia, I became aware of the profound wisdom in the saying, 'It takes a village to raise a child.' After two and a half years nurturing *Optimal Leadership*, it is evident that, although Philip and I have been the primary caregivers, this book's maturation has been a collective communal effort.

I owe an enormous debt of gratitude to the many hundreds of individuals who have played a direct or influential role in shaping the leadership philosophies outlined in *Optimal Leadership*. In particular, I would like to take this opportunity to express my heartfelt appreciation to the following individuals who have generously devoted their energy to the production of this book:

To my darling wife, Judith, thank you for your inspiration (conveyed as 'Please write your stories down so that I don't have to hear them at dinner ... yet again'), consistent encouragement, meticulous proofreading, candid critiques, and delightful illustrations - symbolising the CEO's conducting role.

To our 'children', Constance, Felicity, Gabriella, George, and William, thank you for your painstaking review of the final manuscript and your genuine interest in discussing your father's work.

To Philip Whiteley, for expertly guiding me on this presumably once-in-a-lifetime book creation journey; your support has been indispensable.

To the rest of the team at Breakthrough Books — Emma Allison (cover), Ivy Ngeow (typesetting), Patrick Kincaid (sub-editing), and

Stephanie Bretherton (consulting). Thank you for your professionalism and dedication to this project.

To my former colleagues Andreas Rosenthal, Arjun Mallik, Paul Simons, Sheela Parrakal, and Tan Ping Ping, I appreciate your remarkable wisdom reflected in this book.

To Andrew Scott, for your customary, deeply insightful comments in the Foreword, which have greatly enriched this work.

To esteemed business academics Dean Schroeder, Franziska Frank, Gordon Perchthold, and Vlado Pucik, whose close collaboration over the years has resulted in invaluable endorsements.

To other friends from the business world who have been closely exposed to my leadership and have generously devoted their time to reviewing the manuscript — Abu Addae, Hamish Delves, Jack Chye, Kalai Natarajan, Katherine Xin, Marc Baloch, Michael Diekmann, Phuong Tien Minh, and Sam Luxing — your support has been immensely appreciated.

I am honoured to be part of this village!

Wilf Blackburn

NOTES

1. THE FIRST 100 DAYS

i. Chan Kim, W., Mauborgne R. *Blue Ocean Strategy: How to Create Uncontested Market Space and Make the Competition Irrelevant*, Harvard Business Review 2005

8. AN EMPOWERED ORGANISATION: THE OBSTACLES

i. Pfeffer, J., The *Human Equation: Building Profits by Putting People First*, Harvard Business School Press 1998
ii. The State of the Global Workplace 2023, Gallup, https://www.gallup.com/work place/349484/state-of-the-global-workplace-2022-report.aspx#ite-506897

11. JUST MAVERICK ENOUGH

i. Kohn, A., *Punished by Rewards: The Trouble with Gold Stars, Incentive Plans, As, Praise and Other Bribes*, Houghton Mifflin 1993
ii. Press reports, for example Sam Bankman-Fried pleads not guilty to criminal charges over FTX collapse https://www.ft.com/content/6613eadb-eea0-42f8-8d92-fe46ad8fcf8c

WHAT THEY SAY ABOUT OPTIMAL LEADERSHIP

Professor Vlado Pucik

"Uniquely relevant in today's world of unrelentless tensions facing businesses worldwide, anchored in two decades of CEO leadership experience and personal learning, [Optimal Leadership is] translated into an eminently actionable roadmap on how to deliver results through a highly empowered workforce."

— Prof Vlado Pucik, Visiting Professor Emeritus, Aalto School of Business Helsinki, author of *The Global Challenge: Managing People Across Borders*

Dr Dean M Schroeder

"Reading Optimal Leadership is like sitting down and having a conversation on how to become a great CEO from someone who has been one – in many companies. You get decades of experience in a single read. It will serve as your reference book that you will keep coming back to for practical advice and enduring wisdom."

— Dr Dean M Schroeder, Valparaiso University, author of *Ideas are Free*

Dr Gordon Perchthold

"Aspiring or new CEOs will undoubtedly enjoy greater success after reading this book! Over two decades, I've observed, served, and learned from Wilf's approach to joining, assessing, and rebuilding organisations across multiple companies, countries, and cultures. Unlike most management books that focus on the personal characteristics of successful CEOs, this book takes a different approach. It's a personable 'how-to' guide that pragmatically coaches you on building your CEO skillset to assess, strategise, and facilitate the development of necessary capabilities within your management team and the broader organisation. A book you'll periodically return to for helpful guidance throughout your tenure, navigating the demanding and unpredictable scenarios that arise as a CEO. It's not just about your unique ability to lead as a CEO but, more importantly, your ability to build sustained organisational success through others."

— Dr Gordon Perchthold, University College London, author of *Build and Manage Multinationals for Sustained Growth Across Asia*

Dr Franziska Frank

"I first met Wilf with a group of executives from my business school, and I was greatly impressed by what he said. Not only because they were great stories that participants and I could learn much from about leadership, culture change, dealing with clients etc, but because they also showed Wilf as someone who did not take himself too seriously. When, a few years later, I embarked on writing a book about humility and leadership, I reconnected and had the chance to interview Wilf twice and also speak to numerous people around him. This helped me confirm what I had suspected after the first meeting. Here was a humble manager.

Humility is a trainable virtue that lies underneath/across all leadership behaviour. It consists of four elements. The first has to do with knowing and being able to share one's weaknesses and strengths. The second element is to appreciate others openly – which means that you have to see them first. Thirdly, to always be open to learning, with no fixed mindsets about self and others, and finally, to understand the bigger picture — what I am responsible for and what is due to luck and circumstances.

The charisma of Wilf is obvious and he and his colleagues shared numerous stories for each of the subpoints of humility. So I sincerely hope that any reader will benefit from the stories that Wilf shares and be inspired to walk down the powerful path of humility as well."

— Dr Franziska Frank, Visiting Faculty ESMT (European School of Management and Technology) Berlin, author of *The Power of Humility in Leadership: Influencing as a Role Model*

www.ingramcontent.com/pod-product-compliance
Lightning Source LLC
Chambersburg PA
CBHW071413210326
41597CB00020B/3485